Song of a Stranger

DANIEL

Song of a Stranger

DANIEL

Rico Tice
Peter Maiden
Elaine Duncan
Dave Richards
Elizabeth McQuoid

Authentic

Keswick ministries
bringing the Word alive

Copyright © 2005 Rico Tice, Peter Maiden, Elaine Duncan, Dave Richards and
Elizabeth McQuoid

11 10 09 08 07 06 05   7 6 5 4 3 2 1

First published 2005 by Keswick Ministries and Authentic Media
9 Holdom Avenue, Bletchley, Milton Keynes, Bucks, MK1 1QR, UK
and 129 Mobilization Drive, Waynesboro, GA 30830-4575, USA
www.authenticmedia.co.uk

The right of Rico Tice, Peter Maiden, Elaine Duncan, Dave Richards and Elizabeth
McQuoid to be identified as the Authors of this Work have been asserted by them in
accordance with the Copyright, Designs and Patents Act 1988.

All rights reserved. No part of this publication may be reproduced,
stored in a retrieval system, or transmitted in any form or
by any means, electronic, mechanical, photocopying, recording or
otherwise, without the prior permission of the publisher or a licence
permitting restricted copying. In the UK such licences are issued by the
Copyright Licensing Agency.
90 Tottenham Court Road, London, W1P 9HE

British Library Cataloguing in Publication Data
A catalogue record for this book is available from the British Library

ISBN 1-85078-643-7

Cover design Sam Redwood
Print Management by Adare Carwin
Printed in the UK by Haynes, Sparkford, Yeovil

Contents

The aim of this study guide	vii
Introduction: Rico Tice	3
Chapter 1: What's my line?: Rico Tice	7
Chapter 2: A second-choice life: Dave Richards	23
Chapter 3: Who has your heart?: Elaine Duncan	41
Chapter 4: Facing reality: Rico Tice	55
Chapter 5: 'I'm a Christian, get me out of here.': Dave Richards	75
Chapter 6: The eternal presence: Peter Maiden	93
Chapter 7: The best is still to come: Dave Richards	109

THE AIM OF THIS STUDY GUIDE
In this study guide a number of well-known Keswick speakers retell the story of Daniel, the young Israelite captured during the exile to serve in the Babylonian court. From Daniel's life they show us that it is possible to be faithful to God in a secular culture, that prayer makes a difference and that spiritual integrity matters. The questions in each chapter help relate the principles explained in the commentary to our own lives and situations. You can use this guide either for your own devotional time with God or as a part of a group. Enjoy your study!

USING THIS BOOK FOR PERSONAL STUDY
Begin by praying and reading through the passage and commentary a number of times before looking at the questions.

You may find it helpful to note down your answers to the questions and any other thoughts you may have. Putting pen to paper will help you think through the issues and how they specifically apply to your own situation. It will also be encouraging to look back over all that God has been teaching you!

Talk about what you're learning with a friend. Pray together that you'll be able to apply all these new lessons to your life.

USING THIS BOOK IN SMALL GROUPS
In preparation for the study, pray and read the passage of Scripture and commentary over a number of times. Use other resource material such as a Bible dictionary or atlas if they would be helpful. Each week think through what materials you need for the study – a flipchart, pens and paper, other Bible translations, worship tapes – and read the chapter carefully.

At the top of each chapter we have stated the aim – this is the heart of the passage and the truth you want your group to take away with them. With this in mind decide which questions and activities you should concentrate on. Add questions that would be helpful to your group or particular church situation.

Before people come, encourage them to read the passage and commentary that you will be studying that week.

Make sure you leave time at the end of the study for people to 'Reflect and Respond' so they are able to apply what they are learning to their own situation.

RICO TICE

Based at All Souls Church, Langham Place, Rico has responsibility for evangelism and developed the extremely popular *Christianity Explored* course, which is widely used by groups and churches all over Britain. Rico grew up in Uganda and Zaire and studied history at Bristol University, where he captained the rugby team! His progress towards full-time Christian ministry began with a period as lay assistant at Christchurch, Clifton.

Introduction

How Christian do you think England is today? If you had asked that question in previous centuries, the answer would probably have been that the English did consider themselves to be Christian, on the whole. Most people believed that God existed. Many feared him and toleration referred only to the different denominations on offer. Other faiths seemed far away. They were found in other parts of the world, in far-off lands, and had not penetrated this country. Those were the days of the clergyman in Fielding's *Tom Jones*, who said, 'When I mention religion, I mean the Christian religion and not only the Christian religion but the Protestant religion and not only the Protestant religion but the Church of England.'

We can no longer think of other faiths as only existing elsewhere in the world. It's claimed that as many Muslims go to the mosque on Friday as Anglicans go to the church on Sunday. The coming of other religions, together with the progressive secularisation of our society, has made it increasingly difficult and unfashionable for us to profess and practise our faith today. If we hold to the convictions of our faith then we are far more likely to be called 'judgemental bigots', or 'extremists' or 'fundamentalists' and the words are said with a sneer. Or we may be gently mocked, cold shouldered, or at least politely marginalised and warned.

I've got a friend who's gone into the Foreign Office and he says, 'To be a Christian in the Foreign Office now is seen as career threatening.' Viewing the Christian faith and the Lord Jesus as unique hampers your career prospects.

The mentality of our culture is perhaps articulated best by the philosopher Karl Popper's book, *The Open Society and its Enemies.*[1] That's us – we are the enemies. Christians are seen as that. In his book, Popper argues that belief that one has the truth is always implicitly totalitarian. 'The only safely democratic state of mind', he says, 'is to adopt an attitude of permanent uncertainty about all issues of ideology and world view, because it's a small step from the certainty that says, "I am sure" to the tyranny which says "I must be obeyed"'.

That's how he's thinking; we're the enemy. This mentality hits us at every level. 'How dare you say that the Bible is unique? How dare you say that there is a right way to live?' For example, an unmarried couple come to stay at your home. I have this quite often. Are you going to be so judgemental even to think of putting them in separate bedrooms? How dare you judge their choices, their lifestyle? No, you must apologise for being so judgemental. They don't need to apologise for their promiscuity.

At a dinner party, religion comes up and you're asked your view. You gently explain that the Christian faith says that there is no other way to be forgiven but through the death of the Lord Jesus Christ. Our wrong-doing before God is so serious that it can only be paid for by the death and blood of Jesus. You perhaps don't even push it farther by saying there's only one way to hell – to trample over the cross of the Lord Jesus. You just gently hold up the uniqueness of the cross.

What is the reaction? Fury. 'How dare you, you bigot? What about my sincere Hindu friend?' 'My Jewish neighbour, she's a good woman? How dare you even assert she may be mistaken?' 'You disgust me, you're so intolerant.'

John Stott says 'The road to destruction in our culture is marked by two things – tolerance and permissiveness.' Tolerance – I can think as I please. Permissiveness – I can

Introduction

live as I please. That's what marks the broad road to destruction and we have to stand on that road and say 'Stop!' If you are going to stand up and say those things you may well find yourselves struck off many people's Christmas card list.

In this sort of society there are two main temptations that we face as Christians. On the one hand, we may feel that our country is so hateful of the truth we live by, so intolerant of us, so impure, so far away from the Bible on which it was built, that we have to cut ourselves off, totally. So we retreat from the world into a secure, holy huddle of like-minded people. If you checked out the address books of Christians who think like that, you would find there is no one who do not share their mindset. So many retreat. I work in central London but many retreat there and just live within that network. On the other hand, we can embrace the culture around us so wholeheartedly that we lose any distinctiveness that we ought to have as Christian believers.

The key question emerges: how does God want us to live? Does he want us to renounce our friendships, our networks, our many interests and skills that link us with the world around us so that we can be untainted and purified or does God want us to fit so snugly into our society that no-one notices any difference; we don't live in any way that's different? How should we be living in a society which is increasingly hostile to what we believe?

It's to answer this crucial question, how should we be living in a hostile world, that we're going to turn to the book of Daniel. Daniel was written to encourage believers to continue to trust and obey their God in times when, frankly, it would have been far more comfortable to have been an unbeliever. This book is not to be left in Sunday School – it's for people like you and me, those who are tempted on the one hand to isolation from society and, on the other, to assimilation. The question is, how do we get a godly balance as we face many dilemmas? Where do we stand? Where do we compromise and accommodate? Where do we say, 'I draw the line here'?

There are only two important books in life: my Bible and my diary. The question is, how does this book tell me how to spend my time? How are we to live in this world?

Rico Tice

CHAPTER 1

What's my line?

by Rico Tice

Aim: To decide where to draw spiritual boundary lines in our lives

---

> **FOCUS ON THE THEME**
> If this is the first time your group has met together take time to introduce yourselves. Explain why you have joined this study group and what you hope to learn from these sessions.

Read: Daniel 1:1-21
Key verses: Daniel 1:1-16

THE NIGHTMARE SCENARIO (VERSES 1-2)

Please imagine, as we look at this passage, that we're in the aftermath of the Gulf War in the early nineties, but we have lost to Iraq. We are being transported to live in Baghdad, all of us. So you have to pack your bag and go to Baghdad. You are forced to learn a foreign language, to serve a leader that you loathe, to live in a very alien culture. How would you feel to never see your home and country again? To convey something of the horror of verse

1, think, 'I'm actually going to have to walk the five hundred miles to Baghdad and live there forever.'

Nebuchadnezzar has come to Jerusalem, besieged it and carried its people off to exile in Babylon. It's the first of three deportations. The date is around 605 BC and Daniel is transported to Babylon as a teenager. Eight years later there is a second deportation, after a rebellion in Judah and ten years after that, after yet another rebellion, Nebuchadnezzar razes Jerusalem to the ground and destroys Solomon's temple. If you went through the destruction of your homeland and deportation, what would you do as you walked the five hundred miles to Babylon? I think you'd pray. You'd be praying to the God who had wonderfully given you his Spirit and you'd be saying 'Lord Jesus, please help me in this. This is a dreadful situation. I don't know how I am going to get through this.' If I was having to leave loved ones at home I would need you to pray with me, to comfort me.

That's the real horror and the disaster of verse 2

> And the Lord delivered Jehoiakim king of Judah into his hand, along with some of the articles from the temple of God. These he carried off to the temple of his god in Babylonia and put in the treasure-house of his god.

The Jews believed God had promised them a land. He had set apart this city, Jerusalem, for them. In that city they had built a temple and that was where God was supposed to reside. This was the holy place, the most holy place in all the world that God had given them. They were his people. Surely that would never be taken away? Yet now it's all gone. Why? Because of the folly and idolatry of their leadership. They believed they were invincible. They believed they were God's people. They believed they were his possession and now the nightmare scenario happens –

What's my line?

they are in exile, the temple is destroyed. The temple was where you prayed, so how could you pray now? Could they really take refuge in prayer on the road to Babylon? How could they pray? Weren't they now cut off from God's concern and his purposes? Being exiled either meant God was a wimp and couldn't protect them, so he wasn't in control, or he had finally had enough of them. How could they pray? God was either not sovereign or not interested. No wonder Psalm 137, made famous by Boney M, was sung as they got to Babylon – 'By the waters of Babylon ... we sat down and wept, when we remember Zion'. How could we pray when we have been deserted? They were in total crisis and that is the context here.

Into this crisis, Daniel is raised up as a lighthouse, as a beacon. It's amazing. This young man is raised up as a beacon of faith to his people, to demonstrate that the sovereign God still cares for those who trust in him and obey him, whatever their situation, whatever their nightmare scenario.

When we face nightmare scenarios, we need to remember that God is sovereign and that he cares. We will see that as this passage is unpacked and, above all, we will see that he is in control in the midst of the nightmare scenario.

- *If it is appropriate, share with the group occasions when you have prayed a prayer similar to Daniel's prayer, 'Lord Jesus, please help me in this. This is a dreadful situation. I don't know how I am going to get through this.'*
- *When we face crises we sometimes wonder, 'Is God in control and does he really care?' What questions do you think God would prefer us to ask? In what ways do we need to think differently about our situations for us to ask God the right kind of questions?*

THE PRESSURE TO CONFORM (VERSES 3-7)

Verse 3 tells us that Nebuchadnezzar had a grand plan. He wanted to set up a staff college in Babylon for promising candidates from Judah. Ashpenaz, verse 3, was made Dean of the college. 'Then the king ordered Ashpenaz, chief of his court officials, to bring in some of the Israelites from the royal family and the nobility.' Ashpenaz was only to accept the higher echelons of Judean society. Verse 4 tells us they had to be good-looking, bright and shrewd. He didn't want to waste any of his time with the dim or the gauche. If they graduated with honours after three years then verse 5 tells us they had a dazzling future ahead of them in the king's civil service.

It was a brilliant scheme, to skim off the cream of Judean society, the very people who might be the focus of a Jewish uprising, and harness their talents in the service of the Empire. It's exactly, apparently, what Queen Victoria did. If you look at her Golden Jubilee, in the front row of the Jubilee festivities, are Indian princes, skimmed off from the Indian aristocracy. The aim of the king was to make these men so Babylonian that they forgot their Jewish identity and allegiance to God. Look at their curriculum in verse 4. They would have studied the letters and language of the Babylonians, the superpower. They had languages to learn, new cultures to understand, new clothes to wear. They were even given new names, verse 6, that reflected Babylonian deities, whilst their Hebrew names which testified their allegiance to God were given up. So I arrive in Baghdad and I'm to be called Mohammed. That's what they faced.

It must all have been very enticing to these young men. They'd have seen their country smashed, humiliated. It would have been very tempting to see their future solely

What's my line?

in terms of allegiance to Babylon, the world's superpower. They would have walked round the hanging gardens of Babylon, one of the seven wonders of the world, and said 'This is where I invest my future. This is where the power is. This is where the wealth is. This is where the future for my family is.' They had a bright future, an Oxford place, good prospects of a job in the city, provided they didn't cause any trouble, worked hard and served their new masters with an undivided heart. Perhaps they were like some of us in our offices, being told that promotion, or a directorship, or a partnership, is ours for the taking so long as we turn a blind eye to certain things.

It must have been very tempting for these young men to do what so many do today; to relegate their faith to being purely private, something which has no impact on their careers. I don't know about other churches but at All Souls, my church in central London, our first battle with people who've been at the church for quite a while is sometimes to persuade them actually to tell their colleagues they are Christians. They haven't even stood up on that one. Their faith is a privatised hobby. They are not known as Christians.

No doubt this pressure to conform, five hundred miles away from home, was made all the more tolerable by the quality of the college food. Yet it was on this rather odd matter of college food that Daniel suddenly puts his foot down. He suddenly says 'No.'

- *In what ways do you feel the pressure to conform to secular standards in your workplace, home, school, university, church etc? What subtle and more blatant tactics are used?*

THE COURAGE TO BE DIFFERENT (VERSES 8-14)

Verse 8 is the key verse in the book of Daniel. 'But Daniel resolved not to defile himself with the royal food and wine, and he asked the chief official for permission not to defile himself in this way.' 'But Daniel resolved not to defile himself' – those are the key seven words. The word, 'resolve' is, literally, in the Hebrew, 'he purposed in his heart'. It has the sense of an inner wrestling with conscience resulting in determination to make a stand. Daniel purposed in his heart to make a stand.

- *Daniel wasn't the only man in the Bible to make a resolution. In Psalm 17:3 David resolved not to sin and in 1 Corinthians 2:2 Paul resolved only to preach about Christ. Look at these passages in the Bible and put yourself in the shoes of these two men. What do you think it would cost them to keep their resolutions? What practical measures and further decisions would they have to take?*

It seems odd that Daniel should have chosen to make an issue of the college food. After all, he had not refused to study at the king's college. He hadn't engaged in a student demo at the curriculum imposed on him. He hadn't objected publicly to the new Babylonian name he had been given. What was so special about the food? Shouldn't he have eaten this rich food with gratitude and drunk the wine with gratitude?

Some scholars have suggested that the reason for this protest was that the Jewish food laws prohibited eating certain types of food but that can't be right because Daniel refuses to drink the wine as well. He said 'No' to both. Other scholars have thought that maybe the king's food was offered to pagan idols and that's why Daniel said 'No'. But then the vegetables were probably offered to idols as well. That isn't the reason.

I don't think either of those issues could have been the main one and yet the issue was clearly religious because of the word 'defile' in verse 8. It's a religious word. Daniel didn't want to be corrupted, to be polluted in his faith. So what was the issue? I think that he was influenced by the ancient world's understanding of eating being a sign of friendship. He knew that there was no such thing as a free lunch. It was a sign of loyalty and trust. In fact, in chapter 11:26, we are told that's what it signifies. Those who eat the king's food enter a special covenant relationship with him. That's what Daniel was avoiding.

- *Consider again the pressures to conform you face. Which ones can you go along with and which ones do you think signal a threat to your faith and loyalty to God?*

Daniel knew that he had an exclusive bond of loyalty to just one God, to his God, to the sovereign Lord. He didn't want that loyalty threatened by too cosy a relationship with his pagan master. That's what he was worried about. Perhaps in the midst of such an alien culture with so many temptations to apostasy, Daniel felt that he had to draw the line somewhere as an act of testimony, perhaps to his tutors who felt that they had broken the spirit of these young Judeans.

Perhaps it was also an act of testimony to his fellow students who needed the reminder, as one commentator puts it, that 'Although they would be the king's guinea pigs, they were not his puppy dogs eagerly begging for titbits from their master's table.' I think there is much in that but I suppose the primary thing that motivated Daniel was his own spiritual commitment to his God and to his own walk with God. He knew only too well that he was prone to the enticements of Babylonian luxury. He knew that he was not beyond the pull of the world and at risk of being softened up by the rich food from the king's table. Because of that risk, he said, 'I've got to say no, I've got to draw the line, I've got to nail my colours to the mast at some point.' That was the courage that he showed among his fellow undergraduates. Although it could have easily led to his expulsion from college, even perhaps his execution, Daniel drew this line. That's very brave.

Nebuchadnezzar was not known for his patience. To him, life was cheap. He didn't believe in corporal punishment, he believed in capital punishment. Daniel knew that but still did not wilt in the face of pressure. He still wasn't going to go along with the crowd. Instead he trusted God and trusted his purposes to God. Despite the exile, he was saying 'I believe that God is sovereign and can preserve me through hardships imposed by the Babylonians.'

- *What have been the effects when you have 'nailed your colours to the mast?' How have people responded to you? Has it made living as a Christian harder or easier?*

DANIEL VINDICATED (VERSES 15-21)

This chapter closes with three signs that show that, despite the apparent catastrophe of exile, God is still committed to and able to preserve those Judeans who retain their allegiance to him. We see the first sign in verses 15 and 16. Daniel had proposed to Ashpenaz that he should eat vegetables and drink water. The chief official should test him and see if he was looking any worse after ten days. Daniel is vindicated and instead of looking pale and emaciated, he and his friends 'looked healthier and better nourished than any of the other young men who ate the royal food' (v15).

Secondly, verse 20, God gave great wisdom to these principled young men. Thirdly, and in a way most significantly, look at verse 21, 'And Daniel remained there until the first year of King Cyrus.' This verse is an amazing verse. It means that Daniel survived the entire period of Babylonian captivity. In 538 BC, some 67 years after the events of verses 1 and 2 of this chapter, the Babylonian empire was crushed by the Persian army under King Cyrus and Daniel was still there, preserved. Having as a young man put his head on the chopping block, he was still there. His sovereign Lord had outmanoeuvred the Babylonians.

That's what these three signs are meant to testify to us. Not that God guarantees to rescue us from all difficulty in a hostile world; we know that. I think you know it more as you get older. Life gets harder. It's not that we're rescued from difficulties but rather that God reigns supreme in this world. He was the One who permitted the exile to happen and he is able to preserve faithful servants for the future that he has for them. He alone deserves our trust. We can be encouraged to exhibit the courage of Daniel because of the power and trustworthiness of our great sovereign Lord.

GOD IS IN CONTROL

Let's have a look back through the chapter and see God's control. Verse 2, 'And the Lord delivered Jehoiakim'. God is in control. Verse 9, 'Now God had caused the official to show favour and sympathy to Daniel'. God is in control. Verse 17, 'to these four young men God gave knowledge and understanding of all kinds of literature and learning'. God is in control. And verse 21, 'And Daniel remained there until the first year of King Cyrus'. God is in absolute control.

Lord Reith, the man who set up the BBC, walked into a committee meeting one day and there was silence in the room. He said 'What were you talking about?' Silence. He said, 'What was the discussion?' Silence. Then one person, rather tentatively, said, 'Actually, we have been talking about a series on the death of God and the demise of the Church.' Apparently Lord Reith had a file in his hand and he slammed it on the floor and shouted 'The Church of God will stand at the graveside of the BBC.' Because God is in control of history – he knew that.

In the light of the fact that God is the sovereign Lord, in the light of the fact that he is in control, where do you have to draw the line? Daniel resolved, verse 8, not to defile himself. Do you trust God enough to draw lines in your life? Do we pray this for the young people we know? I've got seven godsons and I've been praying for my seven godsons that they'll be young men who resolve and understand that if you honour the sovereign Lord, he will honour you. 1 Samuel 2:30, 'Those who honour me I will honour, but those who despise me will be disdained.' Surely the reason that Daniel was of use right through his life was because as a young man he learned to draw the line. One commentator said this, 'The older Daniel would never have stood firm in the lion's den if he had not learned as a young man to say "No" to a much more innocuous plate of meat.'

We've got to learn to say 'No' when we are young. We must pray that into peoples' lives. I love Jonathan Edwards. He was a remarkable man, this preacher and theologian from the seventeenth century in American. By the time Jonathan Edwards was twenty-one, he had made seventy resolutions that would enable him to consecrate his life to God. That's why there was a life laid out for the Lord that was so extraordinary in terms of fruit. The question is what pulls us away – alcohol, the opposite sex, money, failing to carve out time to be with the Lord? My boss, Richard Bewes at All Souls, always says that the first hour of the day is the anchor. What we do with the first hour of the day dictates the day. Have we drawn a line there? I've got a colleague who makes sure that in the morning he is ready to leave the house half an hour before he needs to leave, so he has got an untouched half hour to read and pray. Central London, where I work, is extremely difficult in terms of sexual imagery everywhere, even all over the phone boxes. The Sexaholics Anonymous programme say there are two places where people in their treatment cannot go; Amsterdam and London. I have no internet access in my flat, no access to Channel 5 on the television and there are streets and newsagents that I never go to.

If you are an older person, what keeps you away from God? Where has your line got to be drawn? Maybe it's with a very good thing, like family. I spoke recently to a missionary and she was lamenting where her sister was spiritually. She said 'My darling sister is so wrapped up in the children that she has stopped supporting her local church. Mostly, she doesn't even go.' She is so committed to the kids that they've totally taken over, which actually is a desperate example to them.

If you have a career, has the law of advancement become the king's food for you? Over Christmas I was sad to meet a friend and see that he was devoting his waking hours to his work. It was difficult: he had colleagues who were extremely competitive and prepared to work 24/7 but his family and his faith were being sacrificed on that altar.

There are two types of Christian. There are those of us who, when there is a repetitive sin or some laziness or a place where we haven't drawn the line, just stay down on the mat and don't fight. Then there are others who say, 'The Lord Jesus has forgiven me. Lord Jesus, thank you that by your resurrection the Holy Spirit has filled my life. Please help me to battle again.' Are you someone who gets up off the mat or are you staying down? We are not allowed to stay down on the mat. We have to draw the line. It's got to be done.

As I was preparing this message, I spoke to a friend who works in a very intense environment with a pressure-filled job and he said, 'Rico, you've just got to ask people where their line is. Have they drawn one?' He said, 'For my wife and I, at All Souls, it is the prayer gathering and the weekly fellowship groups.' One week we have a prayer gathering and the next week it's a fellowship group, each Tuesday night. He said, 'My wife and I drew the line there. We said, if the job causes us not to be able to attend those meetings, then we will trust the Lord and see it as guidance to change jobs.' And he said, 'That has preserved my spiritual life.' The question is, when did you last make such a resolution?

Daniel had two things going for him as he did this. The first was that he had some friends. By verse 12 there are others with him. There is fellowship, there are other people he can talk to. He is not isolated and he gets help, wisdom and prayer.

Secondly, along with the courage there is also courtesy. Verse 8, 'But Daniel resolved not to defile himself with the royal food and wine, and he asked the chief official for permission not to defile himself.' He doesn't just smash his foot down, go in with all guns blazing; no, he's courteous. He's gracious as he asks permission. He says, 'Do you mind if I don't?' He goes with humility, courtesy and courage. But that we have to draw a line is unmistakable and the Lord Jesus Christ speaks with savage ruthlessness on this issue.

The Lord Jesus is the most loving man that ever lived yet he is savage on this issue of drawing lines. Listen to what he says in Mark 9:43-47

What's my line?

> If your hand causes you to sin, cut it off. It is better for you to enter life maimed than with two hands to go into hell, where the fire never goes out. And if your foot causes you to sin, cut it off. It is better for you to enter life crippled than to have two feet and be thrown into hell. And if your eye causes you to sin, pluck it out. It is better for you to enter the kingdom of God with one eye than to have two eyes and be thrown into hell.

If the Lord Jesus is this ruthless, it's because he knows we are in danger. He loves us enough to lay his life down for us. He says, 'This is dangerous. Draw your line.' Be ruthless. With your feet, don't go there. With your hand, don't touch it. With your eyes, don't look. With your tongue, don't say it. Don't keep going back to that area and speaking of what you mustn't speak. Draw your line and trust the Sovereign God will honour you.

- *Why do we not draw boundary lines? What does a lack of boundary lines reveal about what we think about God and ourselves? For some ideas look at the example of Lot in Genesis 13:5-13, the Israelites in Exodus 32:1-10 and Ezra 9:1-15.*
- *King David was a godly king yet a lustful look at a woman resulted in adultery and murder. Read 2 Samuel 11 – what were the boundary lines that David crossed? How could he have handled his temptation differently?*
- *Do the type of boundary lines we need to draw change as we get older? What has been your own experience?*
- *We're not far into January when we break our New Year's resolutions. How can we ensure we keep the resolutions we make in our hearts to God? How can the church and other Christians help?*

FURTHER STUDY
Read the story of Joseph in Genesis chapters 37–50. How was his life experience similar to Daniel's? What nightmare scenarios did he find himself in? What pressures to conform did he face? Where did he draw the boundary lines and have the courage to be different? How was he vindicated? And how does the story of his life show God's sovereign control?

REFLECTION AND RESPONSE
Take time to reflect on what God has said to you through this study.

- What are the things, even legitimate things, that keep you from total devotion to God?
- Where will you draw the boundary lines? What practical commitments will you take to preserve your exclusive bond of loyalty to God?
- In what particular areas will you have to trust God's sovereignty that he will honour you?

Write these commitments down or, if it is appropriate, share them with another member of the group to help keep you accountable.

Pray for each other that God would give you wisdom, courage and courtesy as you draw boundary lines at home and at work. Pray too that your boundary lines would not only preserve the integrity of your faith but be a testimony to others of your changed life and God's faithfulness.

POINTS TO PONDER
- What have you learnt about God?
- What have you learnt about yourself?
- What actions or attitudes do you need to change as a result?

DAVE RICHARDS

Converted at the age of seventeen through Altrincham Baptist church, David tried for the Baptist ministry but was turned down. He worked for UCCF for three years, leading numerous university missions, before working as an evangelist at St John's Harborne, Birmingham. He then became curate at Knowle parish church, Solihull, before moving to Edinburgh to lead a large, city-centre evangelical congregation at St Paul's and St George's Scottish Episcopal church as their Rector. He also leads a monthly seeker event called 'icon'. He is very keen on sport and supports Manchester United. He loves good holidays and nice wine! His wife Cathy is a consultant psychologist and they have three young children.

CHAPTER 2

A second-choice life

by Dave Richards

Aim: To learn to trust in God's sovereignty regardless of our circumstances

---

FOCUS ON THE THEME
Think back to a time in your life when it was difficult to see God's hand at work: when your circumstances seemed hopeless or a particular dream had been shattered and it was hard to be positive about the future.

How were you able to keep going and keep trusting in God's sovereignty? What helped you the most?

– Having good friends
– Having people to pray with and for you
– Listening to sermons
– Having a regular devotional time
– Receiving practical care from others
– Caring for others
– Reflecting on God's faithfulness in the past
– Taking common-sense next steps
– Other

Read: Daniel 2:1-49
Key verses: Daniel 2:1-29

Central to any relationship is the whole notion of trust. You can't have a friendship without trust: trust is vital. It is the key to any relationship succeeding but trust is in short supply in our society. Trust is at an all-time low: trust in institutions, trust in the media, trust in authority; trust in the Church, trust in politicians; trust between children and parents and parents and children. Over the past thirty to forty years there has been an erosion of trust.

Now in some ways this is nothing new. Twenty years ago, an American student wrote these words:

> We used to trust the generals but Vietnam has changed that. We used to trust the politicians but Watergate has changed that. We used to trust the scientists but the nuclear accident at Three Mile Island has changed that. Now there is nobody left to trust.

The end of the twentieth century was the decade when trust was eroded most in huge swathes of our society; above all, in those under the age of thirty. Cynicism, mistrust and apathy abounds in Generation X, the post-modern generation, the Busters – for whom most relationships seem to have gone bust. The dream of getting better and better has gone bust. The dream of improvement by science has gone bust.

Many of us know what it is to see the erosion of trust – it may have been in the workplace, it may have been in your church, in your marriage, in your family, in a friendship or a relationship. Most of us know what it is to feel betrayed.

The Hebrews in Daniel chapter 2 found themselves in exactly the same situation. They were in a situation where trust had been completely eroded. There had been three invasions of Israel by Nebuchadnezzar, in 605, 597 and 587 BC. Daniel, along with hundreds and thousands of others,

A second-choice life

had been exiled. They had to get used to a new country, a new language, a new leader whom they hated because they had lost the war to him. They had to go and live in Babylon – a whole new world. Many of their hopes and assumptions had been completely blown apart. This was no tinkering with their idea of God; this was no readjustment or realignment of their theology. Things that they had held sacred for hundreds of years were gone, in an instant. Their government had let them down, their army had let them down, even their religion had seemingly let them down. Their view of Scripture and of God, which was completely geared to *their* world, *their* culture and *their* desires being fulfilled, had let them down.

All their assumptions had been completely shattered. The Hebrews at this time had several assumptions. The first was that the royal line of King David would continue uninterrupted until the second David, the Messiah came. The second assumption was that Israel would triumph and be the centre of a new world commonwealth. Then, thirdly and crucially, Jerusalem and the temple would stand free and invincible. Now it wasn't just a dream that lay in tatters. Jerusalem had been burned, the temple razed to the ground, and hundreds of thousands of them taken away in exile.

They were in prison, they were homeless, they were homesick and they were without hope. Things looked hopeless and what they needed was a new theology for a new context, a new situation and a new reality. They needed a theology that, in spite of all that they saw around them, somehow held out hope for the future; a theology that affirmed God's sovereignty, even in the face of events all around them – and all around us. We are in a very similar situation. For many of us, the givens and the assumptions that we grew up with are no longer visible in our society. Society, in the last fifty years, has undergone tremendous changes. We live in a society that now thinks that a personal, living God is dead; where I rule me because nobody else has the right to. We exist in a society where there is no such thing as absolute truth – what's true is what's true for me. 'You go to church on a Sunday, I go to B&Q. It's the same thing, isn't it? At least the people at B&Q are friendly.' We live in a society where there is no such thing as a common morality, where consumerism reigns and community dies. The truth is that we are a people in exile, we are a church in exile and just like the people of Israel, we need a new theology of hope, because many of our hopes, our assumptions, have been blown apart. We need that theology of hope, a theology that affirms God's sovereignty even in the face of all that surrounds us.

- *To what extent do you think 'we are a church in exile'? Give specific examples of Christian values and assumptions which are no longer accepted by contemporary society – and the effect this has on how we think and behave as Christians.*

We too, if we are honest, as good Bible-believing evangelical Christians may feel that our view of Scripture, our religion and even our God, have betrayed us and left us without hope. I don't know what situations you are facing in your life, what have been the biggest challenges for you and your faith. I can remember, in my last church, praying for a three-year-old who had cancer; praying for him for over a year and then seeing him die. The parents, congregation and I were left with questions. *Why? Why didn't God answer our prayers the way we wanted him to?* We couldn't figure it out. We prayed in the right way, or so we thought, and lots of us prayed. Somehow God didn't answer the way we expected. And I, like many people in that church, if we are honest, felt a sense of betrayal.

A second-choice life

You may have been in a similar situation. One of your children, whom you have prayed for, may be miles away from God. A particular job situation that you prayed about didn't work out the way you hoped. An illness strikes a friend or family member and things go completely opposite to the way you'd thought, hoped, dreamed and expected. A marriage implodes and you are left thinking, where was God?

The question for you and me is the question that came to Daniel. In this church in exile, surrounded by a society that is alien and at times hostile to the Christian faith, how can we cooperate but not compromise? How can we engage, like Daniel, but not be engulfed? How can we influence but not be infiltrated? How can we be distinctive and remain relevant?

- *What are the particular issues your church is facing as it tries to maintain its distinctives and be relevant to the local community?*
- *How does having a theology of hope and affirming God's sovereignty help us deal with these difficult situations?*

A DICTATOR AND HIS INSECURITY (VERSES 1-13)

> In the second year of his reign, Nebuchadnezzar had dreams; his mind was troubled and he could not sleep. So the king summoned the magicians, enchanters, sorcerers and astrologers to tell him what he had dreamed (v1,2).

It is a curious quirk of history and humanity that if you look at the biographies of all the world's dictators, Napoleon, Hitler, Stalin, even Saddam Hussein, they have all demonstrated incredible power but also incredible insecurity and anxiety. Stories abound of their cruelty, their petty jealousy and their pride, and Nebuchadnezzar was no different. In chapter 2 he's in the second year of his reign; he was powerful, popular and respected. He was victorious in battle and popular at home; he ruled an enormous empire, from Egypt to the Euphrates. Babylon was becoming a wonder of the known world, a city of learning, wisdom and beauty. Nebuchadnezzar was also gaining a reputation as something of a philanthropist, a benefactor, an architect and a builder. But now he starts to be niggled by his dreams.

Dreams in that culture were respected as communications from the spiritual world and so Nebuchadnezzar was worried, verses 2 and 3. 'When the astrologers came in and stood before the king, he said to them, "I have had a dream that troubles me and I want to know what it means."' And the astrologers say, because this is what they always said, verse 4, 'Tell your servants the dream, and we will interpret it.'

Nebuchadnezzar might be insecure but he wasn't daft. He knew that they had a dream manual, a sort of *Dreams for Dummies*: it was well known in different cultures that they had this manual. There was an Egyptian version and this was the Babylonian version. *Dreams for Dummies* came with standard explanations for dreams. So if the person had a dream about *a*, the standard explanation was *b*. If someone had a dream about *x*, then the standard explanation was *y*. So the king used his nous. He gave them a challenge – verses 5 and 6.

> This is what I have firmly decided: If you do not tell me what my dream was and interpret it, I will have you cut into pieces and your houses turned into piles of rubble.

He obviously came from the incentive school of management!

> But if you tell me the dream and explain it, you will receive from me gifts and rewards and great honour. So tell me the dream and interpret it for me.

We're not told but I would guess that verse 7 comes with a nervous giggle. 'Let the king tell his servants the dream, and we will interpret it.' Then the king answered, 'I am certain you are trying to gain time, because you realize that this is what I have firmly decided: If you do not tell me the dream, there is just one penalty for you ... So ... tell me the dream' (vs 8-9).

In verses 10 and 11, by now perhaps panic-stricken, they say 'Nobody can do it! Tell us the dream, meet us halfway, Nebuchadnezzar. You tell us the dream and we will give you the interpretation.' Nebuchadnezzar is not for moving. Verse 12:

> This made the king so angry and furious that he ordered the execution of all the wise men of Babylon. So the decree was issued to put the wise men to death and men were sent to look for Daniel and his friends to put them to death.

THE IMPORTANCE OF PRAYER (VERSES 14-19)

Daniel's response is interesting; tact and time. Daniel spoke with great courtesy in chapter one: now he uses that same courtesy again as he responds with tact (v14) and asks for time (v16). I was helped a few years ago when somebody said to me 'Remember that time and truth walk hand in hand.' What happened in a particular situation will be seen to have happened. Don't try to force the issue, don't try to hurry things along but just trust that time and truth walk hand in hand: truth will out.

Daniel is a remarkable young man. His abilities of communication, tact and diplomacy, wisdom and spirituality were rooted in his character, not in any expertise he had picked up along the way. He asks in verse 15 'Why did the king issue such a harsh decree?' Daniel did not ask the favourite question most of us ask when we get bad news; 'Why me?' Daniel asks 'Why has the king issued this decree?' and his response, very simply, is to pray (vs 17, 18).

> Then Daniel returned to his house and explained the matter to his friends Hananiah, Mishael and Azariah. He urged them to plead for mercy from the God of heaven concerning this mystery, so that he and his friends might not be executed with the rest of the wise men of Babylon.

Faced with this situation, Daniel knows that it is only God who can help him and that he needs to listen to God. Daniel believes that things happen when he prays and that God will hear and act. This is a reminder these Hebrews in exile desperately needed to hear, that the God they had put their trust in, the God they believed in, that they had prayed to for so many years, was the same God who was able to hear their prayers and to respond.

It is possible that some of us need to be reminded of that. If we're honest, prayer is not our first response when we hear bad news. It once was but now it isn't because one day we prayed and the heavens seemed like brass. No answer came, and the answer that did come was the opposite of the answer that we requested. Maybe we need to be reminded that God does hear our prayers. That child you have prayed for, for years, and who is still not a Christian – God has heard your prayers. Keep on praying, keep on loving, keep on hoping, keep on believing.

- *Why is prayer not more of a priority for us? How can we recover Daniel's urgency in prayer?*

There is a lovely story of an eighty-year-old woman on her deathbed. The vicar went to see her and said, 'What

A second-choice life

about your two sons, are they Christians?' And the woman replied, 'Not yet.' Even though her life was in its final chapter she still believed. If you want a book to help you think again about prayer and how it fits with the world you're in, read Viv Thomas's *Second choice*.[2] It's one of the most helpful books and it happens to be on Daniel. It asserts that, for most of us, we live life in a second-choice world. The job that we have, the family life we've got, the relationships we've got, etc, are often not our first choice, they're our second choice. Very helpfully, Viv Thomas explains how Daniel's second-choice life and his prayer life fits with his relationship with God. Some of the most helpful things I have ever read about prayer in twenty-seven years of being a Christian come from this book.

Viv Thomas writes:

> It is in prayer that we are most fully ourselves. People gather before God, responding to their Creator. It is through prayer that we start to engage the large dimensions of our reality and without it we are destined to live our lives in smallness.

Those of us who have given up on praying – if we look at our lives, our hopes, our ambitions, what occupies most of our time – we are destined to spend most of our time in smallness. Thomas goes on

> Prayer releases the imagination and creativity that we need in times of crisis and engagement with our second-choice world. Wisdom, understanding and revelation come to us as we submit ourselves to God and allow him to initiate what he will.

It strikes me that Daniel is prepared, indeed Daniel is desperate, for God to answer his prayers, but he remembers the prayer may not always set up the answers that he wants. But it does set up the conditions for us to respond to whatever answers we get.

One final quote from Thomas

> Prayer, like most conversations, gives us the perspective to see what is going on, even though we cannot control all the circumstances.

I was reminded of those words a year ago last January. I was about to take the kids to school and I was just flicking through Ceefax in that thirty seconds before my eldest dragged me off because he didn't want to be late. He's type A and I'm type B and he tries to get me there on time. And flicking through the news pages of Ceefax, I saw that a policeman had been shot and killed in Manchester.

Twenty-six years ago, there were two teenagers in a youth fellowship in a church just south of Manchester. One came from a very strong Christian family. The other one was clueless. The one that was clueless was me. I didn't pay much attention to this newcomer from the south of England. My only concern was that he seemed very friendly with the girl that was my girlfriend. What made it even more alarming was that his Dad was a police officer and I knew that she wanted to be a police officer and I knew that this other teenager wanted to be a police officer too. We weren't best friends but we knew each other, we went on youth group weekends away, so imagine my horror when I stood in front of the TV screen and realised that the name of that police officer was the same as the name of that teenager that I knew; Stephen Oake.

I remember watching the news that night, when his father, Robin, spoke. He is a remarkable man. He's about six foot five, and when he says 'Pray', you pray! When I knew him he was Assistant Chief Constable of Greater

Manchester and he went on to become Chief Constable of the Isle of Man. Robin spoke very simply on that news bulletin, saying that he was praying for Steve's family, for his daughter-in-law and his grandchildren, but most amazingly of all, that he was praying for the man who killed Steve. Robin, in the midst of that situation, was trying to get perspective and strength through prayer, because it is as we draw close to God that we see things as they really are and get an inkling of the fact that God is in control after all and that somehow God is walking alongside us.

I will never forget a woman called Judy who came on an Alpha course a few years ago. She had come back to faith through the course, and the night that we spoke about healing and the work of the Holy Spirit, she suddenly broke down in tears and sobbed. My wife and I, who were leading her small group, tried to help her and said 'It's okay, God is with you now.' She looked at us through tear-stained eyes and said, 'I know he's with me now, that's the whole point. There were all those years, all that pain, and all those tears. I faced them alone and it didn't need to be like that.' She realised that God was there with her but she had never turned to him and she had never acknowledged his ability to help her and give her strength.

- *What are we saying to God when we keep praying even though our circumstances do not improve?*

DANIEL NEEDED PEOPLE (VERSE 17)

Daniel needed to pray, but he needed people. His response wasn't to go away and pray by himself, but to go and find his three closest friends and to pray with them. Daniel, this visionary, extremely intelligent, skilled politician and man of prayer, needed other people to pray with him.

Jesus, another visionary, gifted, committed, man of prayer and Son of God, needed other people to pray with him. Isn't it striking in the Garden of Gethsemane that Jesus takes along his friends? He knows that they are going to fall asleep, that they won't be much use praying but he needed to have their physical presence just a few yards away from him. He needed friends. So if Daniel needed friends to pray with, if Jesus needed friends to pray with, why do we feel that we are any different? Why do we think that most of the verbs in the New Testament apply to us individually? That somehow this Christian thing is about me and God, rather than us and God?

It is said, all too often, to people who feel lonely in church, 'You need to put your trust in God. God is there for you and he is all you need.' I was struck by one of the worship songs we sing. It's a great song but I'm not sure of the theology of one of the lines. The line is, 'You are all I need'. This may be heresy, but it strikes me as interesting that before the fall God looks at Adam and says 'It is not good for man to be alone'. If ever there was a man who could be told, 'Look to God, he is all you need', it was Adam. He was in a perfect relationship with God, but God looked down on Adam and said it was not good for him to be alone and provided a helper for him.

I want to apologise to those of you who have ever been told by a church leader, a minister, a counsellor, a homegroup leader, or another older Christian, no doubt sincerely, earnestly and meaning the best, simply to put your trust in God because God is all you need. I don't think that is biblical because God provided a friend for Adam. Jesus came from community, the Trinity, and he said 'Wherever two or three people gather in my name, I will be there.' It's as if Jesus just can't resist being with people when they gather in his name, because he loves friendship and he loves community and he can't stay away.

A second-choice life 35

- *Why do you think that in the West Christians have become so individualistic and self-absorbed?*
- *How can good friends and pastoral care help us through difficult circumstances? What are their limitations?*

PRAISE TO GOD (VERSES 20-23)

The answer that comes to Daniel is this amazing interpretation of the dream, as well as the dream itself, and what pours out from Daniel in verses 20 to 23 is praise to God. He praises God that he is everlasting, he praises him for his nature, verses 20 and 21; for his sovereignty and his power, verses 22 and 23. The good news for Daniel and for us is that there is no darkness, no riddle and no mystery that God cannot understand and reveal to us.

ACTION IS NEEDED (VERSES 24-29)

Finally, it isn't always enough to pray (vs 24-29). Prayer is crucial, praying with other people is crucial, but they are not the end of the story. For Daniel there had to come a time when he acted, verses 27 and following. There had to come a moment when Daniel went into Nebuchadnezzar's presence and spoke what God had said and once he did, Daniel's world and Nebuchadnezzar's world would never be the same again. It was a very significant moment for Daniel and also for Nebuchadnezzar. Look at verse 47 – Nebuchadnezzar suddenly sees who God really is

> Surely your God is the God of Gods and the Lord of Kings and a Revealer of mysteries, for you were able to reveal this mystery.

Acting on an answer to prayer, Daniel changed his and Nebuchadnezzar's world for ever. All because he had three friends to pray with. Daniel prayed, Daniel praised and Daniel acted because he knew the importance of friendships. I wonder whether we do.

- *We may not always hear God's response to our prayers as loud and clear as Daniel did, so how can we be sure that we're acting as he would want us to? Describe what it means to 'act trusting in God's sovereignty'.*
- *What thoughts or ideas have challenged you most from this week's study?*

FURTHER STUDY

Read Daniel's description and interpretation of the dream in 2:31-45. Consider how commentators have dealt with this passage. Some helpful commentaries to consult might be:

The Bible Speaks Today – Daniel – **Ronald Wallace**[3]
Expositors Bible Commentary – **Volume 7** – ed. Frank Gaebelein[4]
The NIV Application Commentary: Daniel – **Tremper Longman III**[5]

What would the dream have meant to King Nebuchadnezzar? How would the dream have encouraged the first Israelites who read Daniel's account? What are the timeless truths we can gain from the dream and what difference should they make to our lives?

REFLECTION AND RESPONSE

Spend time in personal reflection:

- Do you have two or three friends to pray with, whom you can be yourself with? Can you be honest with them and can they be honest with you?
- Do you believe that God has or will hear your prayer? Or do you not believe God will respond any more?

A second-choice life

- Has God told you something, and now you need to act? Maybe at work or in a relationship, God has given to you the responsibility to respond.

As a group of exiles are there particular issues in society, politics, the media or your locality that you need to pray about or take specific action on?

POINTS TO PONDER
- What have you learnt about God?
- What have you learnt about yourself?
- What actions or attitudes do you need to change as a result?

ELAINE DUNCAN
After studying for a psychology degree, followed by a brief spell on the nursing staff team in a psychiatric unit, Elaine worked for UCCF for fourteen years before moving to Glasgow to work for Scripture Union Scotland as Regional Activities Director. The focus of Elaine's work has always been the gospel amongst young people. One of her greatest joys is to see people (of any age!) gain a fresh insight about God through his word and to grow in their relationship with him. Elaine particularly loves savouring the beauty of God's creation, and walking up the hills of the Lake District and Scotland is her favourite way of enjoying it! Elaine is a Trustee of the Keswick Convention.

CHAPTER 3

Who has your heart?

by Elaine Duncan

Aim: To grow in our hearts' devotion to God

FOCUS ON THE THEME
Jesus replied ' "Love the Lord your God with all your heart and with all your soul and with all your mind." This is the first and greatest commandment. And the second is like it: "Love your neighbour as yourself." All the Law and the Prophets hang on these two commandments.' (Mt. 22:37-40)

Consider these two commandments. What do you find most encouraging/most difficult about them? What gets in the way of obeying them? What hope and help does Jesus offer us as we strive to be obedient?

Read: Daniel 3:1-30
Key verses: Daniel 3:1-18

What is the greatest and most important commandment? It is 'Love the Lord your God with all your heart, all your soul and all your mind.' And Jesus went on to say, 'This is the first and the greatest commandment and the second is equally important. Love your neighbour as yourself.' All the other commandments and all the demands of the prophets are based on these two commandments.

'Love the Lord your God with all your heart, all your soul and all your mind.'

Jesus is asked which is the greatest commandment twice in the gospel records and he asks it once himself of someone else. Each time the answer is the same. We can be sure that this is indeed the greatest commandment. This chapter of Daniel is about that greatest of all commandments. In it we find one man, Nebuchadnezzar, who fails to keep that commandment and three men, Shadrach, Meshach and Abednego, who obey it.

Chapter 2 ends with King Nebuchadnezzar saying 'Surely your God is the God of gods, the Lord of kings and a revealer of mysteries, for you were able to reveal this mystery' – the secret of his dream. Nebuchadnezzar had had this insight into the glory and character of the Living God. But it does not last. In chapter 3, Nebuchadnezzar goes on to live the next phase of his life obviously connecting somewhat with the dream; quite taken with this idea that he is the head of gold but not quite grasping the whole point of the dream. We find Nebuchadnezzar believing his own publicity, becoming something of a celebrity in his own eyes. We don't know whether the statue he has built is a statue of himself or whether it's of one of the local deities, one of the local gods. His motivation, the commentators suggest, is probably something to do with social cohesion, bringing about a certain togetherness. Here he is with his own people, the Babylonians, who've been victorious in battle and have taken captives from the surrounding nations, including the Israelites, and it's almost as if Nebuchadnezzar now says, 'Let's get all these people from all these different backgrounds to have a common role for their worship. Let's get them worshipping the same god.'

It seems to be a little like football in Britain today, something that gathers people together. Something that says, 'Let's focus all our time and energy and resources into this one thing and this will bring us social cohesion.'

Every one was to bow down in front of this statue. When he talks about all the musical instruments that are to be the signal that this worship is to start, it sounds a bit like the Notting Hill Carnival. This was a real event in the nation. This was something that was to bring togetherness and a focus to the people. But what it certainly brought was a pressure to conform. The expectation was that everybody would join in. In fact, it wasn't just an expectation; it was an instruction and there was a severe penalty if you didn't.

THE SEDUCTION OF IDOLATRY

The human heart, that is, the totality of who we are, everything about us, heart, soul, mind, body, is made to worship. The first commandment to love God with everything that we are is there because it is the only safe way to be a human being. We are built to worship. We are built to adore. We are built with the passion, the emotion and the creativity to put into adoring and worshipping someone or something else. It's part of how we are made as humans. But we are only truly human when all that we are, body, mind and soul, is focused into worshipping the living God, the One who has created us; the One who, alone, is worthy of worship and adoration. He is the One who alone is glorious in splendour, majesty and holiness; the One who is the Creator; the One who is in control of the world that he has made. Worship is part of our lives. The question is, whom will we worship?

Despite Nebuchadnezzar recognising God as being Lord over kings, he has not humbled himself before God. He, again, has become king of his universe. His pride has swung him back into being the centre of his world. He had that glimpse of the reality, the truth about life, the universe and everything, but then he lost it again. It strikes me that it must be quite hard for a king to be humble; the position that they have, the servants, the people around them who are there to look after all their needs. It must be very hard for a king to be humble. But I have to confess it's very hard for me to be humble.

As Christians, when we read this chapter, we tend to put ourselves in the Shadrach, Meshach and Abednego group. They're God's people and we're God's people, so we tend to align ourselves with them. We don't quite like the sound of a fiery furnace but we hope that we would be the heroes; that we too would have the courage to stand where they stood. But if I'm honest, I think I'm more like Nebuchadnezzar. I like to be centre of my world; the lord and queen of my universe. I need to allow God's Spirit to shine his spotlight on my paths and in my life. I hope you will be open to do the same. We need to allow the Spirit to show us where we are being idolatrous.

Think about the New Testament and the gospels when Jesus encounters the Pharisees. I always prick up my ears when reading anything about Jesus and the Pharisees because it seems to me I would have been a Pharisee; loving God, keen on his word, wanting to know his word, wanting to live a life of holiness. I would have been right in there doing my best to keep the rules and regulations. I need to be very alert when Jesus speaks to the Pharisees.

When Jesus spoke to the Pharisees, he had to use stealth bombing methods because they thought they were fine. They thought they were sorted. It's often when the Pharisees are around that Jesus tells parables, and they're the stealth bombs of the gospel, of Jesus' teaching, because they take the Pharisees unawares. They are the only way that the Pharisees can be brought face to face with their own idolatry. That is how I need God to deal with me and

Who has your heart?

I hope it's how you allow God to deal with you. We need to be open to the subversive tactics of the Holy Spirit, if that is what it's going to take, to show us where we are worshipping someone or something other than the living God who alone is worthy of our worship. We are so easily seduced away from loving and worshipping God.

Idols abound in our society. You probably don't need me to tell you what some of the accepted idols are in our twenty-first-century Western culture. There's materialism; what you have is what matters, it defines you. Our national debt in the UK has apparently reached £1 trillion. That's a 1,000,000,000,000. If you are anything like me you can't get your head round those big numbers. It boils down, I have it on good authority, to £17,000 per head of population; every man, woman and child. You can't say we're not a materialistic society.

Individualism is another idol of our time. 'I have rights, not responsibilities', is the resounding message of individualism. I believe that the increases in sexual promiscuity and litigation are both connected with this idolising of self, of me, of my rights. 'Everything that matters is to do with my happiness', that's what individualism says. 'I am the one that matters.' There has been an incredible increase in sexually transmitted diseases, not just among young people, although frighteningly so, but also amongst older people. We are an increasingly promiscuous society where everybody thinks that the thing to do is the thing that pleases them, with no thought to anyone else. And the other big idol of our time is relativism. Truth no longer matters. The new god to be worshipped is tolerance.

We need to think how these things affect us within the church. Think about materialism. A few years ago, John White wrote a book that originally came out under the title *The Golden Cow*[6] and then was republished under the title

Money isn't God – so why is the Church worshipping it?[7] I believe that book is still as relevant today as it was twenty or thirty years ago when it was written. Our individualistic and solitary lives, that say 'This is my life and no-one else has any say over how I live' affect our churches, where we have lost the strength of community. We have lost that sense of commitment and belonging to one another. We talk about 'joining a church' as if that is our choice. God chose you and he put you in his family and you belong to God and you belong to God's people around you. We need to recapture, particularly in the church in the UK today, something of the strength of that community commitment and genuine belonging to one another that comes from being God's people.

When faced with relativism, we have to see that the truth about Jesus Christ matters. In the church today we have lost our confidence. We may be afraid, but we must be able to say graciously that Jesus and Jesus alone is Lord and Saviour.

- *In what other ways are materialism, relativism and individualism seen in the church today?*
- *Why have these idols become so accepted within the church?*
- *If these idols were removed, what would the church look like? What would be the hallmarks of a church fully devoted to God? How does your church need to change to fit this description?*

So how do we spot idolatry in ourselves? We do need to allow the Holy Spirit to shine his spotlight but I think our part is to be courageous enough to allow him to do that and to be honest enough to face the reality. Jeremiah said, 'It's the heart that is deceitful above all things.' We need to believe that. However long we have been Christians, we need daily to allow God's Spirit to search our hearts and to check out where they belong.

Maybe some questions that help us to think about idolatry in our lives would be, 'What do I spend my time thinking about?' What about those moments when your brain goes into free-fall – what do you settle on or think about in those times? What do I spend my money on? What do I spend my time doing? What warms my heart and stirs my emotions? Idolatry is a matter of passion, love, adoration and devotion. It's a heart matter. It's expressing something very deep within us and that is why it's only safe to worship God.

How would you feel if you were to show another Christian your bank statements? Not just the cash withdrawals but what you then spent that cash on? What about a detailed diary of your time? What about a history of the websites you'd visited? How would you feel about showing that to someone else? There's something in us that says, 'That's my business.' Why? Who gave you your money? Who gave you your resources? Who gave you time? We're not our own; we were bought with a price. We need to help one another to make sure that it's the Lord who has our hearts, our wallets, our time and our minds. Who or what has your heart? God didn't have Nebuchadnezzar's heart – yet.

- *Where do you recognise idolatry in your own life?*
- *There are many things that legitimately occupy space in our hearts – our family, spouse, friends, ministry, work – so how do we practically give priority to loving God? How can we love God wholeheartedly and juggle all these other commitments at the same time?*

RESISTING THE PRESSURE TO CONFORM

What do we learn from these three heroes in the story, Shadrach, Meshach and Abednego? What helped them take this firm stand in the light of this incredible threat to their lives if they didn't conform?

They knew their identity

They knew who they were because they knew whose they were. They knew whom they belonged to. They were keeping the first commandment. They were loving and worshipping only the living God. They knew what it meant to be properly human. Their hearts were filled with the love of God. He was the source of their work and their boundaries and their understanding of themselves.

Identity is something we struggle with. I work with young people and teenagers and repeatedly the conversations we have are about who they are. Often their behaviour, the most odd sort of behaviour, is about trying to discover who they are. The hair colour that they turn up to camps with and the clothes that they wear are attempts to discover who they are. It seems to me that this is a cry of so many people in our society. We are desperate to know who we are. We are quite insecure people. Even those who come across as arrogant and very sure of themselves are often masking a deep-rooted uncertainty about who they really are.

Nebuchadnezzar's aim was to make these Israelites into good Babylonians, hence the rigorous training programme, the depersonalising of them by the change of name and re-programming into a new culture. They were in real danger by not conforming. We sometimes think that we're in real danger if we don't conform, if we don't fit with the crowd, if we don't go with the flow in our society. But for Shadrach, Meshach and Abednego, their identity was beyond the

Who has your heart?

reach of Nebuchadnezzar. He couldn't get at that. They knew they belonged to the living God; the God who involved himself in human affairs; the God who isn't just out there beyond us; the God who is right here, with us.

We have to ask ourselves 'Are we secure enough in God and in our Lord Jesus Christ to be beyond the influence of what others use to define themselves?' Where does our worth and identity come from? The people around us so often find it in their jobs, their marriages, their children, in the house they live in, the car they drive, the clothes they wear, all the wrong places. And we do too. Is our identity secure in God? Daniel and his friends knew their identity was secure; they knew that they belonged to God.

- *What are the tell-tale signs that our jobs, marriage, children, house, car and clothes are giving us a sense of self-worth and identity?*
- *Explain how being sure of our identity in Christ helps us resist idolatry.*

They lived wisely

These friends of Daniel are Israelites in Babylon and that's a problem for them. They have been robbed of all the outward expressions of their faith and their religion. The temple is destroyed, Jerusalem lies in ruins, the priests are no longer doing their job. And they cry, 'How can we sing the Lord's song in a strange land?' You'll find that in Psalm 137. God is teaching them how to sing his song in a strange land. He is teaching them how to live as his people in their pagan environment. They are beginning to learn new lessons, the lessons that Jesus was trying to teach the Pharisees; the lesson that outward, external human rules have absolutely no power to transform us. In our churches today I suspect we live as if they do.

Shadrach, Meshach and Abednego knew that they were dealing with issues of the heart. What if we had been there? What would we have done in order to survive as God's people in that environment? I suspect, and I'm only surmising, that we would have developed rules. We would have hedged ourselves in with those things that we definitely were not going to do. Now to some extent, Daniel and his friends do that. But if we had been there, would we have felt that Daniel and his three friends had gone a bit too far in getting into this new culture? Would we have felt uneasy about the way that they were rising on the career ladder and getting into positions of influence alongside Nebuchadnezzar and his successors? Would we have felt uneasy about how they were living? Were they still God's people?

It seems to me that in the evangelical church today we have got ourselves into legalism. We've got ourselves trapped with rules and regulations. Think about your church. What are the rules about how to be a good church member? Think about your home. What are the rules there about how to be God's person? We live with rules and in the church we often make the rules equate with God's law. And they don't. The law that these men were grappling with was clearly God's law, an issue of the heart and of worship. Very often we add human rules and regulations because we think they protect us from idolatry. But they don't. External rules cannot protect us from idolatry.

I wonder whether we are teaching our children and young people that we want them to love God, to be humble and to be merciful? Or are we teaching them that when you are in church, you keep quiet and you don't run up and down the aisles and you don't climb on the pews, if you still have them? Are we communicating to our children that we want them to be those whose hearts are absolutely devoted to the living God and that is far more important than having a tidy room or doing their homework?

Who has your heart?

Human rules and regulations are very dangerous. That's why we have to listen to what Jesus says to the Pharisees. We like rules, because with a little bit of self-discipline we can keep them. We can tick the boxes; yes, we've done that. But when we live like that, we actually distance ourselves from God. The Bible is not a book of rules. It is a book of law but that is different. God's law keeps us humble because we can't keep it. We need God. We need his grace. We need his mercy. The way that we will be protected from idolatry is to humble ourselves before God and ask for his wisdom about how we should live, rather than imposing on ourselves and on one another human rules and regulations.

- *'The way that we will be protected from idolatry is to humble ourselves before God and ask for his wisdom about how we should live.' In what ways does God reveal his wisdom to us? How do we find his wisdom for living?*

With children and young people, we want to help them grow in wisdom, and in order to do that we don't give them the details of what they should do, because that doesn't help them mature. You need to give them guidelines because you want them to imitate character, not copy actions, so that they develop maturity and wisdom. I think that is something of what God wants to do with us. It would begin to transform some of our relationships and certainly some of our churches if we grasp what it means to love God with all of who we are.

They live in expectation

Verses 16-18

> Shadrach, Meshach and Abednego replied to the king, 'O Nebuchadnezzar, we do not need to defend ourselves

before you in this matter. If we are thrown into the blazing furnace, the God we serve is able to save us from it, and he will rescue us from your hand, O king. But even if he does not, we want you to know, O king, that we will not serve your gods or worship the image of gold you have set up.'

They knew that God would turn up. But they knew it in such a way that they weren't prepared to dictate what God would do when he showed up. He might have shown up by taking them through the fiery furnace, through death into his presence. He didn't. He showed up in the fiery furnace and rescued them from the fiery furnace: not *before* it, but while they were *in* it. They had this incredible trust in a God who acts and a God who does things, a God who is at work amongst his people. 'Those who honour God, he will honour.'

God is for us. It's demonstrated here as he rescues Shadrach, Meshach and Abednego from the furnace. It is demonstrated absolutely for all of us, much more fully, in the coming of Jesus Christ and his death on the cross for each of us.

Do we believe that God will show up in the nitty-gritty details of our lives? And what difference would it make if we really believed that? What would your life look like if you believed that God was going to show up? We can't dictate what he will do but we can trust him with our very lives. What is the greatest commandment? 'To love the Lord with all your heart.' Will you live expecting God to show up?

- *If you loved the Lord with all your heart what difference would this make to:*
    - *How you deal with the mundane aspects of life?*
    - *Your aspirations and expectations for the future?*
    - *How you cope with anxieties and difficulties?*

- *Your relationships?*
- *Your perception of ministry?*
- *Your dedication to work?*
- *Your willingness to be part of the church community?*
- *Your identity and sense of worth?*
- *Your responsiveness to the Holy Spirit?*

FURTHER STUDY

The command to 'Love the Lord your God with all your heart ... ' is repeated in the Old and New Testaments because God cares deeply about the focus and condition of our hearts. Look up the following Scriptures to see what God has to say about your heart. What does he say to you if:

1. You are broken-hearted (Ps. 34:18, 147:3)

1. You are faint-hearted (Deut. 20:3-4)

2. You need to take heart (Ps. 31:24, Jn. 16:33)

3. You need encouragement not to lose heart (Heb. 12:3-6)

4. You want to be pure in heart (Mt. 5:8)

5. You want to refresh another's heart (Philm. 1:20)

REFLECTION AND RESPONSE

God searches us and he knows us. In silence consider, 'Who has my heart?' 'What is holding me back from wholehearted devotion to God?' What ways of thinking or habits do you need to surrender so that you can say with the apostle Paul 'God, whom I serve with my whole heart ...' (Rom. 1:9). Take time to renew your commitment to God.

When God has our hearts we want to worship him. Shadrach, Meshach and Abednego were willing to worship God whether he rescued them from the furnace or not. They knew God's presence and his commitment to them as the fourth man walking around in the furnace. Like the three friends, we have Jesus' presence with us in our troubles, as we try to stand against idolatry and as we resist conformity to our secular culture. But like the friends, we have also been rescued. Jesus' death on the cross was the greatest rescue mission ever. As a group, worship God for his presence with you now through the Holy Spirit but also for the salvation that he has won for us through Christ. Pray, read Scripture, and sing songs or hymns. If it is appropriate, remember how costly our rescue was by sharing communion together.

POINTS TO PONDER
- What have you learnt about God?
- What have you learnt about yourself?
- What actions or attitudes do you need to change as a result?

CHAPTER 4

Facing reality

by Rico Tice

Aim: To appreciate the reality of Christ and how he defines our world

> **FOCUS ON THE THEME**
> What are the realities that shape your life? What are the non-negotiables that dictate your daily routine and influence your decisions and priorities? Perhaps it's the need to pay off the mortgage, to get the children to school on time, to have a daily devotion or to attend the house group. Make a list of as many non-negotiables as you can. How do you think your list would differ from a non-Christian friend's list?

Read: Daniel 4:1-5:31
Key verses: Daniel 5:1-31

Jesus can sometimes be a very distant figure in modern life. His name is frequently heard in our films but only as a curse. Last night, as I was going to bed, I saw the start of the golf film, *Tin Cup*, and Kevin Costner's opening words in the film are a curse using Jesus' name. The discussion programmes covering the big issues of the day never even acknowledge Jesus as the central figure in the universe. They refuse to begin with the fact that underpins all of life. Colossians 1:16-17 says 'For by him all things were created: things in heaven and on earth, visible and invisible, whether thrones or powers or rulers or authorities; all things were created by him and for him. He is before all things, and in him all things hold together.'

So there is wave upon wave of shared ignorance and delusion because people haven't got the fundamental reality of Jesus Christ in place. There is so much desperate ignorance, such a lack of wisdom. Religion goes on about some kind of god but ignores the one who actually is God, who has clearly revealed himself. God is not hiding, he has come and revealed himself, he's risen from the dead.

The news stories come and go, focused only on the world of human affairs but never keeping us informed about the real news, the news of the proclamation of Jesus Christ in his world. That is the real news that will last for eternity. The songs are written and sung, the films are made and watched, the newspapers are compiled and sold and they all seem to be caught up in a fantasy world where the Son of Man, who sustains and rules the universe, who gives us each breath, is ignored. It is outrageous.

Jesus Christ, the Son of Man, lived among us. He taught as no-one has ever taught. He healed as no-one has ever healed. He passed through death into immortality as no-one has ever done. He had total authority over nature and over death. He calmed the seas, he raised the dead girl, and yet there is a massive and deliberate pretence that he is not who he manifestly is. This is the irony in which we live. What is called 'the real world' is a fantasy deliberately cut off from the person who defines reality.

- *Why do people ignore Jesus and his claims?*
- *How does Jesus define reality for a non-Christian even if they don't acknowledge him?*

My church, All Souls Langham Place, is right next door to the BBC in the West End of London. I've been there ten

Facing reality

years pursuing my ambition to be the longest serving curate in the history of the Church of England. It's going well, because I find after ten years, incompetence is the key. They just don't promote you. I don't mean to boast but I would like you to know that in the last ten years I've been asked by the BBC to speak three times. The three subjects they have asked me to speak on have been 'The Christmas Lights', 'Hermits' and 'Transvestites.' Now which one of those three do you want to speak on? I will only be asked to speak on that which allows the media to represent the Christian faith as weird and judgemental. I'll only be allowed to give credence to the metanarrative, the overall story, that has been created in society and which allows our culture to live with the assumption that Jesus Christ lived a long time ago and anybody who wants to follow him must do so in the privacy of their own home. If you want to follow him, that's fine but do it in the privacy of your home. It's a private, rather odd, antiquated belief; a hobby akin to croquet.

What is right at the heart of human sin, of human rebellion? Romans 1:18 tells us, 'The wrath of God is being revealed from heaven against all the godlessness and wickedness of men who suppress the truth by their wickedness.' God's personal hostility to evil is revealed against those who suppress the truth about Jesus. Any of us involved with small people can understand this. I've got two nephews, Dalton and Patrick, they're eleven and nine. I'm not even those boys' father, I'm just their uncle but I'm so emotionally committed to those boys that if you ignored them, or you cut them dead, or you hurt them in any way, we would be enemies.

Let's put that on a cosmic scale. God has made the world through his Son, Jesus Christ. We rebelled again him. He then sent his Son, the Lord Jesus, to die. Right at the heart of sin is ignoring Jesus. He said in John 16:9 that the Holy Spirit would come and convict men 'in regard to sin, because men do not believe in me'. The heart of sin is ignoring Jesus Christ. That's not an intellectual decision, that's a sin and we all have charming, polite friends who do exactly that and they're right at the heart of sin. There is, perhaps, no better example in the whole of the Bible of a man who in his wickedness and godlessness suppressed the truth about reality than King Belshazzar in Daniel chapter 5.

It is a chilling story. This man did not just inherit an empire, he also inherited the story of King Nebuchadnezzar. Nebuchadnezzar was strutting around on his palace balcony looking down, boasting 'Is not this the great Babylon I have built as the royal residence, by my mighty power and for the glory of my majesty?' But amazingly four verses later, (Dan. 4:34), having been dramatically humbled over seven years of madness, he looks up to heaven and confesses the key truth of chapters 4 and 5 – 'I, Nebuchadnezzar, raised my eyes toward heaven, and my sanity was restored. Then I praised the Most High; I honoured and glorified him who lives forever.'

Belshazzar didn't just inherit an empire and inherit this truth of King Nebuchadnezzar; he also inherited Daniel, the teacher of this truth. He inherited a man who could help him to understand how to live in the light of reality. And what is reality? It's in chapter 4:17, chapter 4:25, chapter 4:32 and chapter 5:21. It is the reality at the heart of these two chapters. 'The Most High is sovereign over the kingdoms of men and gives them to anyone he wishes.'

- *Who or what have you inherited to teach you the truth about the reality of God? Who or what is there to help you understand how to live in the light of that reality?*

Belshazzar must understand that all human authority is delegated by God. The BBC, next door to me, don't understand that. A royal crown is but a gift from God. No king is able to be independent and autonomous without eventual accountability. That was the lesson Nebuchadnezzar learned in chapter 4 and the reality Belshazzar denies in chapter 5.

THE PARTY (VERSES 1-4)

Verse 1 of Daniel 5, 'King Belshazzar gave a great banquet for a thousand of his nobles and drank wine with them.' It's 538 BC, twenty-four years after King Nebuchadnezzar has died and we know that Belshazzar is living in a fantasy world because of verses 30-31. 'That very night Belshazzar, king of the Babylonians, was slain, and Darius the Mede took over the kingdom.' A week earlier, Darius had defeated the Babylonian army some fifty miles away and the account in Herodutus tells us that now, ten days later, his army was encircling Babylon. It was on all sides. What would Darius do? Would he raze the city to the ground? Would he capture it? Would he send a diplomatic mission and create a vassal state?

Imagine yourself to be Belshazzar, the ruler of Babylon, in that situation. What would you do as king? Check your defences, send for reinforcements, visit the troops to lift morale, plan a strategy with your generals? Verse 1, this is what the fantasist does. He gets out the Chateau Babylon to eat, drink and be merry with a thousand nobles. That's an extraordinary military strategy. Was it a nervous reaction? One last fling before defeat? Was he trying to bluff his opponents? Did he think he was invincible? We don't know, but we know that this party began to get out of hand. Drinking is mentioned five times in the first four verses. It's like the worst type of rugby post-match function; people trying to dare each other with more and more reckless acts and you're sitting there, thinking as a

Christian, 'The coach isn't going until 11, it's 8.30 and they're behaving like animals. What am I going to do?'

Then Belshazzar, whilst discarding another winebottle, has an idea which no-one else could possibly upstage; verses 2-4

> While Belshazzar was drinking his wine, he gave orders to bring in the gold and silver goblets that Nebuchadnezzar his father had taken from the temple in Jerusalem, so that the king and his nobles, his wives and his concubines might drink from them. So they brought in the gold goblets that had been taken from the temple of God in Jerusalem, and the king and his nobles, his wives and his concubines drank from them. As they drank the wine, they praised the gods of gold and silver, of bronze, iron, wood and stone.

These are the goblets Daniel mentions in chapter 1:2 when he describes the stripping of the Lord's temple in Jerusalem. We read 'And the Lord delivered Jehoiakim, king of Judah into Nebuchadnezzar's hand along with some of the artefacts from the temple of God. These he carried off to the temple of his god in Babylonia and put in the treasure-house of his god.'

Of all the things for the author to mention, as the temple is destroyed, he mentions these artefacts. Nebuchadnezzar had gathered up the religious articles from the magnificent temple in Jerusalem and stored them in his own temple as trophies. Belshazzar thinks, wouldn't it be fun to dig out those old cups so that he and his friends and all their lovers could drink from such exotic artefacts? What a novel way to toast his gods who were the theme of the party and what a vivid way of pouring scorn on old Nebuchadnezzar's strange faith in some Jewish Creator God. Let's get out the artefacts and have a

Facing reality

few drinks. So he takes what belongs to God, what was meant to honour God, and mocks him by honouring other gods instead.

It's a deliberate act of public contempt; not least because these golden goblets were stored on the table of the Presence in the temple of Jerusalem, located right at the centre in the Holy Place; right in the middle. In Numbers 4:7 we read that these goblets were used for drink offerings which consecrated the priests for service. Out of these goblets, wine or blood would be poured and that would cleanse the priests. Furthermore, the great Messianic hope, the Lamb of God, would be exalted as the wine was poured out. To treat these cups with ridicule was to treat the Messiah with ridicule. The cups were also there to look ahead to the great Messianic banquet at the end of history which showed that the Messiah held history in the palm of his hands. Here they are, using them as sacrilege. Can you imagine? You've got to have one toast for each god, for gold, silver, wood, stone. Each would require a drunken refill.

In my first year of playing rugby at Bristol University, I was playing against an army side at Shrivenham. After the match there was lots of drinking and singing and it got more and more rowdy as various drinking games were played. Then there was a very weird moment because a soldier got up on a table and he called for calm. There were eighty people in this bar but he got silence and then he began to sing. It was extraordinary for me. I was nineteen, recently converted and I had never heard anything like it. He sang 'There is a green hill' in a wonderful, melodious tenor voice. 'There is a green hill far away, without a city wall. Where my dear Lord was crucified and he died to save us all.' I was just staggered as I heard this, until twenty-five soldiers, all with beers in hands, came rocketing in with 'For he's a jolly good fellow, for he's a jolly good fellow, for he's a jolly good fellow, and so say all of us.' And they howled with laughter at the crucifixion of the Lord Jesus. It was a terrible moment. They mocked the cross, they mocked the rescue. That is exactly what Belshazzar is doing here.

- *In what ways does our society mock the reality of God and show public contempt for him?*

THE PARTY ENDS (VERSES 5-12)

This is the most famous piece of gate-crashing in history. Verse 5, 'Suddenly the fingers of a human hand appeared and wrote on the plaster of the wall, near the lampstand in the royal palace. The king watched the hand as it wrote. His face turned pale and he was so frightened that his knees knocked together and his legs gave way.'

So the drinks were poured, the laughter and shouts went on, the music played, the entertainment continued and then, like a meteor crashing into a busy street, the real owner of the temple cups brought the entire party to a deadly silence. Suddenly reality breaks in. There is an objectivity that crushes the place as the atmosphere in the room goes from a drunken orgiastic feast to the feel of an execution chamber, in one moment. There is the menace and confrontation of a human hand writing words that no-one understands on the wall. Can you imagine the terror of a human hand writing across the air? The dreamworld of Belshazzar's feast has received a message of reality, a word from eternity, a sentence of judgement. Matthew Henry, the great eighteenth-century Bible scholar, makes this comment, 'The king saw part of hand that wrote but saw not the person whose hand it was which made the thing more frightful. If this be the finger of God, what is his arm laid bare and what is he?'

Facing reality 63

Faced with this, the man who is so keen to display his contempt for God was reduced to a blubbering wreck. His knees knock, he can't control himself and there is almost a hint of comedy as the man who thinks he rules an empire cannot rule himself. In his panic, verse 7, he calls for enchanters, astrologers, and diviners and he tries to restore his world of normality where he is back in charge. He offers gifts and honours and the third highest place in the kingdom to 'Whoever reads this writing and tells me what it means' (verse 7). 'Then all the king's wise men came in' (verse 8). They're rather like one of these idiotic choruses in a Gilbert and Sullivan comic opera. They could not read the writing or tell the king what it meant. Verse 9, 'King Belshazzar became even more terrified and his face grew more pale.'

The queen mother, Nebuchadnezzar's widow, takes charge with calm authority. She's not his wife, we know that because the wives are already in the banqueting hall. She's almost certainly the queen mother because she walks uninvited into the presence of the king. She remembers the years of Nebuchadnezzar's early reign. She remembers her husband's sleepless nights. She remembers his disturbed dreams. She knows the disembodied hand is not just a trick of thought, it's not just an alcohol-induced hallucination and in her husband's day there had been only one man in the kingdom who could interpret such visions. Mercifully he was still alive. An old man, now discredited and pensioned off.

> The queen, hearing the voices of the king and his nobles, came into the banquet hall. 'O king, live forever!' she said. 'Don't be alarmed! Don't look so pale! There is a man in your kingdom who has the spirit of the holy gods in him. In the time of your father he was found to have insight and intelligence and wisdom like that of the gods. King Nebuchadnezzar your father – your father the king, I say –

appointed him chief of the magicians, enchanters, astrologers and diviners. This man Daniel, whom the king called Belteshazzar, was found to have a keen mind and knowledge and understanding, and also the ability to interpret dreams, explain riddles and solve difficult problems. Call for Daniel, and he will tell you what the writing means.'

THE PROPHET SPEAKS (VERSES 13-24)

In some ways, this story has echoes of the story of Joseph in Genesis 41, where Joseph is forgotten until a crisis erupts. Daniel is not in prison but he is forgotten until there is a crisis. Often I think that's the case for a parson these days, forgotten until a crisis erupts and then people who ignored God suddenly make a phonecall.

Nevertheless, the king's anxiety is so great that he's willing to consult anything and anybody. In verse 13 and 14 we see that Daniel's CV is impressive. The king opens the file and the résumé is all there. Verse 13, 'Are you Daniel, one of the exiles my father the king brought from Judah? I have heard that the spirit of the gods is in you and that you have insight, intelligence and outstanding wisdom.' Then Daniel, having been pensioned off during the pagan renaissance, gets offered the usual carrot. 'Help me and you'll get promoted to a cabinet secretary and one day, there'll be a seat in the House of Lords for you.' I don't know what a guy in his late eighties would be interested in that for, but that was the offer.

However Daniel, God's prophet, is not in it for cash. He doesn't want the money. In verse 17 he makes it absolutely clear that divine wisdom cannot be bought. 'You may keep your gifts for yourself and give your rewards to someone

Facing reality

else. Nevertheless, I will read the writing for the king and tell him what it means.'

Daniel gives us flashbacks and edited highlights from Nebuchadnezzar's reign to make it clear that (end of verse 21), 'the Most High God is sovereign over the kingdoms of men and sets over them anyone he wishes.' Belshazzar should have known. It had all been told him, he was privy to all this information in verses 18-21.

> O king, the Most High God gave your father Nebuchadnezzar sovereignty and greatness and glory and splendour. Because of the high position he gave him, all the peoples and nations and men of every language dreaded and feared him. Those the king wanted to put to death, he put to death; those he wanted to spare, he spared; those he wanted to promote, he promoted; and those he wanted to humble, he humbled. But when his heart became arrogant and hardened with pride, he was deposed from his royal throne and stripped of his glory. He was driven away from people and given the mind of an animal; he lived with the wild donkeys and ate grass like cattle; and his body was drenched with the dew of heaven, until he acknowledged that the Most High God is sovereign over the kingdoms of men and sets over them anyone he wishes.

Do you see the drama the narrator weaves in? Nebuchadnezzar has his pride inflated by his military success and his narcissistic pride grows. He succumbs then to a devastating mental breakdown but in the middle of that breakdown, in the midst of his insanity, God is real to him and God grants him remission and he is humbled and categorically states that the sovereign God is Lord of all. He says, 'My empire will now live with this reality. As the papers are published, the *Daily Babylon Times*, it will have this reality at the centre.'

That's what he commands and Belshazzar knew all this. But now Daniel makes it clear that Belshazzar's problem was not ignorance but arrogance, verse 22. It's a terrible verse. Verse 22, 'But you his son, O Belshazzar, have not humbled yourself, though you knew all this.' Belshazzar had refused to learn. He knew these events were no myth circulating among the Jewish community. He knew the extent of Nebuchadnezzar's power, how he had been humbled by the Most High God and yet he thought he could take on God himself. Verse 23-24

> Instead, you have set yourself up against the Lord of heaven. You had the goblets from his temple brought to you, and you and your nobles, your wives and your concubines drank wine from them. You praised the gods of silver and gold, of bronze, iron, wood and stone, which cannot see or hear or understand. But you did not honour the God who holds in his hand your life and all your ways. Therefore he sent the hand that wrote the inscription.

'You did not honour the God who holds in his hands your life and all your ways.' That is the verdict on Belshazzar and not just on Belshazzar but on much of the world today. It's the verdict on London, it's the verdict that thunders into our society with all the cycle of news, discussion, religion, entertain, sport, finance, glamour and education. The absence of the Most High God and his Messiah is the most glaring feature in our world and we are no longer outraged by this. We actually do believe that our faith is a personal privatised thing, practised behind closed doors, and that our dear neighbours will not stand before this God in eternity. So we are functional universalists. We say we believe there is a judgement to come but we don't, because otherwise we would speak to our friends and neighbours. But we put the conversations

Facing reality

off again and again and then we go to their funerals. We say, 'It's very sad' and yet we know that they've lived their whole lives right at the heart of sin, which is to ignore the truth of the Lord Jesus Christ and his cross. We are functional atheists, otherwise we would speak to these dear people for whom Christ has died. We have shut him out of our normal lives, so have our neighbours and we don't seem to care. 'You did not honour the God who holds in his hands your life and all your ways.' That is the verdict.

- *Consider what Daniel said to the king in verses 22-23. Often the same accusations could be levelled at us. Why is it that even as Christians we refuse to accept the reality of God and how he defines the world?*
- *In what ways can we begin to share the truth of the Lord Jesus with others if we are not naturally outgoing or gifted evangelists? Share practical ideas with each other.*
- *Consider the following scenarios – what would it mean to honour God and bring the truth of Jesus Christ to these situations?*
  - *You are the only Christian in your home. Your spouse has become less interested in God and the church over the past few years and now refuses to even talk about God. Your children have also decided they are not coming with you to church.*
  - *You are a mother at home with small children. How do you honour God in your context? How do you teach your children now, and as they grow, about the truth of Jesus Christ?*
  - *There are only a few other Christans in your office. You have explained about your faith when people have seemed interested. But apart from sharing the gospel, are there any other ways you bring God's truth to the work place? How else can you honour God in the office?*

- *What about your own situation? How can you honour God and let the truth about Jesus Christ make a difference in your sphere of influence?*

I've got a friend and she teaches seven and eight-year-olds in Northern Ireland. One day she said, 'Make a world.' These little people laboured all morning. They made people, houses, roads, animals, pools, gardens and parks. Then she said, 'Now I want you to write something called a constitution which is the rules by which these people should live.' And these little kids sat around and they very seriously drew up a constitution on how these people were to treat the world they had made. At the end of the day she said, 'How would you feel if the people you have made decide that they are going to live their lives their own way and pretend that you, their creators, don't exist?' One quiet, mild little girl scrunched up her face and said, through gritted teeth, 'We'd rip their legs off.'

Fortunately, the God who holds our life and our ways in his hands is far more patient and merciful. But, as Robert Lewis Stevenson wrote, 'Everyone, sooner or later, sits down to a banquet of consequences.'

THE JUDGEMENT COMES (verses 25-31)

Here is Daniel interpreting the godly graffiti.

> This is what these words mean: *Mene*: God has numbered the days of your reign and brought it to an end. *Tekel*: You have been weighed on the scales and found wanting. *Peres*: Your kingdom is divided and given to the Medes and Persians.

These words are the names of small weights that would have been used in the market place and the underlying

Facing reality

thought is that there is going to be an assessment. The balance of divine justice is going to be weighed up. The royal plasterwall in the palace resembles a gravestone and this is Belshazzar's epitaph. It's some epitaph: '*Mene*, your days are numbered.' Your credit limit has been reached. Our days are numbered, our opportunities are numbered. Psalm 90:12 says, 'Teach us to number our days aright that we may gain a heart of wisdom.' As an Anglican clergyman, you stand at the graveside and you say these haunting words over the grave, 'As for man', Psalm 103, 'his days are like grass. He flourishes like a flower of the field; the wind blows over it and it is gone, and its place remembers it no more.' Life is so short, our days are numbered.

I spoke recently with a woman whose husband is in Iraq, doing a very dangerous job. I said, 'How are you coping with the worry?' and she said, 'God has numbered my husband's days. I just don't know what that number is but I am trusting the sovereign Lord.' I thought that was a good answer. There is someone who believes in the sovereignty of God.

This is ultimate reality. Your days are numbered. How are you using them?

Verse 27, '*Tekel*, you have been weighed on the scales and found wanting.' His rebellion counted very heavily against him. The eternal Judge will weigh us and give a verdict. Belshazzar's life had been examined on the scale of eternal reality. I don't think there is anything that people who live their lives without reference to God hate more than this. The reality of the resurrection of Jesus means not only that God raised him but it's the promise that the coffin is not an exitless box. You and I will be raised and judged. There will be a resurrection body for all at the judgement to come. The life to come breaks into this life and we will be raised and judged and our days will be weighed.

- *What is your response to the reality that your days are numbered and they will be weighed by God the eternal judge?*

'*Peres*, your kingdom is divided and given to the Medes and Persians.' It's very stark. But God says, 'I am your appointed executioner and will remove you and your kingdom.' Belshazzar is suddenly to be sent out of the dream world in which he has lived into reality.

Yet verse 29 is extraordinary. The writing's on the wall and he still thinks it's playtime. 'Then at Belshazzar's command, Daniel was clothed in purple, a gold chain was placed around his neck, and he was proclaimed the third highest ruler in the kingdom.' Now what should Belshazzar have done? Having had a death sentence like that proclaimed against him, he should have been flat on his face. That's what Nebuchadnezzar modelled. Nebuchadnezzar said, 'Listen, you don't mess with this God. Now get down on your face.' He had realised that. Belshazzar won't do it. He carries on as normal. He stands on the edge of a deadly precipice about to come crashing down on the judgement of God and still he pretends he is king and showers goodies on a reluctant Daniel. Can you imagine Daniel wandering back to his quarters with the gold chain on him, taking if off, throwing it in the bin?

Belshazzar does nothing but give Daniel gifts. We are not told how the king spent the rest of this evening. Does he go back to the party? Perhaps he retires to bed with his favourite book. I don't know. But by verse 30, it seems, he's gone to bed and his fate is sealed. 'That very night Belshazzar, king of the Babylonians, was slain.' And can I say, this is the fate that will befall all who rebel against this God. What the Old Testament touches on, in earthly terms, the New Testament completes in eternal terms. The Bible says this, 'He will punish those who do not know God and do not obey the gospel of our Lord Jesus Christ. They will

Facing reality

be punished with everlasting destruction.' All rebellion will be overthrown, it will be paid for. That is reality.

In the centre of London is the Old Bailey, the home of British justice and, on top, is Pomeroy's golden statue of Justicia. She stands blindfolded, with the sword in one hand and the scales in the other. The sword is the sword of wrath and the message of British justice is clear, 'If you are found wanting in the scales, the sword will fall.' But just across the skyline is St Paul's Cathedral and there is the golden cross. That cross says, 'Yes, the sword of God's justice did fall but it fell onto Jesus Christ.' So either we let him pay for our sin on the cross or, like Belshazzar, we pay for it ourselves in hell.

If, at the beginning of Daniel, you'd gone down to Ladbrokes and placed a bet, do you reckon you'd have bet on these Israelite boys that came five hundred miles from Jerusalem? Do you reckon you'd have bet on them surviving in a strange land, standing up and standing out? And then on a king being converted? And the next king being judged? It only happens because of the sovereign Lord. It happens because Jesus is king. The whole of reality revolves around him because, in him, all things hold together in a culture that puts us in exile. You may have a pagan boss, or a pagan teacher, or a pagan colleague, whatever it is but the Lord is King and he humbles who he wants to humble. He has got the whole world in his hands and because he is the King, our job is to stand for him, graciously but to stand for him and to live in the light of that reality. That is the reality we live with. Everything else is dreamworld.

- *Scan through Daniel chapter 1, 2:14-28, 4:19-27, 5:13-30 noting how Daniel responded to the various difficulties he faced. What do we learn from him about how having a grasp of reality can shape our response to our circumstances?*

FURTHER STUDY

Writing to the Colossians believers, Paul urges them to live in the real world and not be trapped by fantasy, legalism and false theology. He tells them plainly that 'the reality… is found in Christ' (Col. 2:17).

Take time to read through the book of Colossians. What can we learn about:

- The reality of Christ and his work in the world
- The reality of our salvation
- The reality of how we should live in the light of these truths

What are the main ways you have been encouraged and challenged by this book?

REFLECTION AND RESPONSE

Jesus is reality and our world is defined by him, but even for Christians the struggle is to appreciate this and live in the good of it. Our attitude needs to be the same as John the Baptist, 'He must become greater; I must become less' (Jn. 3:30). In silence, consider:

- How can I make Jesus more of a reality in my life?
- What aspects of 'self' do I need to discard?
- In what ways am I living in a fantasy world?
- In what ways should I be alerting others to this fantasy world?

As a group, pray that God would give each of you the opportunity to share the reality of Jesus with one other person this week. Keep remembering each other in prayer and be ready to report to the group how you got on.

POINTS TO PONDER
- What have you learnt about God?
- What have you learnt about yourself?
- What actions or attitudes do you need to change as a result?

CHAPTER 5

'I'm a Christian, get me out of here.'

by Dave Richards

Aim: To examine the impact of our witness in the workplace

> **FOCUS ON THE THEME**
> You may know the other group members quite well but still not know much about each other's work life. Explain to the group what your work (what you spend most of your time doing) involves – it could be looking after a home, attending university, being in an office etc. What part of your work do you most enjoy? How easy is it to be a Christian in your workplace?

Read: Daniel 6:1-28
Key verses: Daniel 6:1-23

The person over the past four or five years who has challenged and inspired me most on the subject of Christianity in the workplace is Mark Greene. If you've never heard him or if you have heard him and would like to remember what he said, then why not get *Thank God it's Monday*[8] which is one of his books. It looks at what it means to be a Christian in the workplace. It's the contention of many people in Britain that what Mark is saying to the church, at the moment, is as prophetic as what John Stott said to the church in the 1980s about listening both to the word and the world. God is using Mark Greene to speak to the church in Britain about our attitude towards witness and our lifestyle in the workplace.

Many of us have grown up with the attitude that work is just something that gets in the way of being a Christian. Our picture of heaven is such that we think it's going to be one long Keswick Convention. The tent may be bigger, the worship group might be better, the speakers will definitely be better but it certainly will not be one long church service. Work was given to humanity before the fall and the bad news is that work will also be there in heaven. God will have work for each of us to do. But the way in which we organise our lives as Christians and as churches doesn't often reflect the importance that God gives to work.

- *What does the creation account in Genesis 1:26-2:2 teach us about God's view of work?*
- *Why do you think we don't generally share God's perspective of work and see it instead as 'something which gets in the way of being a Christian'?*

One of the things that Mark Greene says is that in the prayer life of our churches, we have a league table of importance. At the top are those of us who happen to work and be paid to work for a church; clergy, ministers or church leaders. Number two, just beneath them, are missionaries. If you work abroad, you're higher up the prayer league table than those who are missionaries at home in the UK, because the work's more difficult. Then below missionaries are people who work for Christian organisations; administrators, people who perhaps work in finance or charities. Then, because Mark Greene used to be the Vice-Principal of London Bible College, he puts

Bible College principals. And because he used to be an advertising executive, he then puts advertising executives. But people who make money because of their work certainly don't merit prayer. Stephen Rand, who worked for Tearfund, said that he used to work as a teacher in his local comprehensive surrounded by hundreds of people who weren't Christians and he was never prayed for once. Then he went to work for Tearfund and was prayed for every month. Maybe it said something about the people who worked at Tearfund, that they needed more prayer than the people in the school.

About eighteen months ago I was involved in getting Mark Greene to come and speak at a conference in Scotland, addressing the whole subject of evangelism. We asked him to take one of the preliminary sessions and to speak about being a Christian in the workplace. Mark said in all the years that he'd spoken at conferences, this was the first conference where he'd been given a keynote session to talk about being a Christian in the workplace. At all the other conferences the subject had been relegated to a seminar or a workshop slot. At the end of each day of the conference we videoed people and asked them about their experience and we then presented a video diary. The day after Mark Greene spoke, one of the people who was interviewed, a Church of Scotland minister, very committed to Scripture, said these words on the video, 'For twenty years before yesterday, I thought the church members existed to support my ministry. Today I realised that I exist to support church members in their ministry.' Here was somebody who was well versed in Scripture, who knew Ephesians 4, probably in the Greek, but had missed the point. The reason God gives gifts, some to be apostles, pastors, teachers, evangelists, is to equip God's people for works of service that they might be equipped for works of ministry.

It is still my dream that at St Paul's and St George's in Edinburgh, we will have a notice board one day outside that says 'St Paul's and St George's Church, Edinburgh: Ministers: the whole congregation.' That is a biblical picture of ministry. We may not be called overseas but even if we're not, you can guarantee that each one of us has been given a mission field. That mission field is where we live and where we work. And if you think about the amount of time that you spend at work, maybe that should be your primary place of witness and evangelism.

- *What would you do differently, how would you act differently, if you genuinely regarded your workplace as a mission field?*
- *What could your church do to support you in your ministry in the workplace? Come up with some practical suggestions for how 'work' could be given a higher profile in your church.*

Mark Greene also came and spoke at our church weekend away. It was a great weekend, inspiring and challenging, again on the subject of being a Christian in the workplace. But on Sunday morning a very awkward moment occurred. Mark asked people to get into small groups depending on occupation, depending on the sphere that we spent most of our time working in. It was very enlightening. Being the only person who was paid to work for a church, I was in a small group of one and therefore was able to stand and watch people wrestle with this whole area. They had had one and a half days of talks on the subject but this was a huge shift of gear. There were about two hundred people and it took them ten minutes to get into small groups. It was fascinating to see that we had so many computer people in our church who, when we'd made appeals for help with our computers, had never responded. It was fascinating to see that being the type of church we are, we had few plumbers: none in fact. It was also fascinating to see that in the corner where those people who worked for the NHS were gathering, the doctors were refusing to meet with anybody else who worked in the NHS. They wanted their own group. The surgeon also wanted to be in a group by himself.

Why did it take so long and why was it such a struggle for church members to get into small groups? Because they didn't want to label themselves, in the church context, by their jobs. There's a very good reason for that: in our society, we value people by profession and salary. Doctor Lee Salks, a psychologist, said, 'People jockey to find out what each other earns because in our society, money is a symbol of strength, influence and power.'

Work forms a big part of our life. In the UK over a quarter of people work more than forty-eight hours a week. Apparently twenty per cent of all manual workers work more than fifty hours a week. One in eight managers work over sixty hours a week. And interestingly seven out of ten people want to work no more than forty hours a week but only three out of ten people do. There are huge changes in the work scene. Forty million people now across the world now have e-mail and the number of secretaries has declined by twenty per cent in the past ten years because people now do their own administration and send their own letters. Work has changed dramatically and it will carry on changing.

Warren Bennis has been one of the great gurus of management and leadership in the United States for the past twenty or thirty years. He said, 'The factory of the future will only have two employees: a man and a dog. The man will be there to feed the dog; the dog will be there to stop the man touching the equipment.' We live in a situation, a culture, a work environment, where things change dramatically and quickly. For many the change is bewildering and confusing and the questions come thick and fast. What does it mean to be a Christian in the workplace? Is ambition biblical or not? Which is more important, secular work or so-called church work? Can secular work ever be God's work? How do you avoid being swallowed up by the culture that you live and work in? How does a Christian deal with making someone else redundant? As a Christian should you react differently if you are made redundant? Have you ever had to think through these questions?

● *What are the current issues at work that are challenging your Christian faith?*

Daniel chapter 6 gives us a few pointers. It's the famous story of the lions' den, a great favourite of Sunday school teachers but with real relevance for adults. Perhaps for too long we've allowed Sunday school teachers, important though they are, to hijack this story. We've got used to seeing children with lion masks, we've watched video after video that was aimed at children and we've lost the application for us; people who are supposed to be grown-ups.

The situation that we pick up in Daniel 6:1 has changed. At the end of chapter 5, Belshazzar king of the Babylonians was slain and Darius the Mede took over the kingdom, at the age of sixty-two. There's a new king in Babylon. Darius the Persian comes to power and (v 1) 'It pleased Darius to appoint one hundred and twenty satraps to rule throughout the kingdom, with three administrators over them, one of whom was Daniel. The satraps were made accountable to them so that the king might not suffer loss.'

THE NEW MANAGEMENT STRUCTURE (VERSES 1-2)

With the new king comes a new management structure. There are three administrators, one of whom is Daniel, over a hundred and twenty satraps and officials. There's a hint already at the end of verse 2 that these satraps might not be the people they would like other people to think they are. There's the possibility that the king may suffer loss because the satraps are going to say one for you and about ten for me. Corruption is there and that's important. In verse 3 another new management structure appears because Daniel impressed Darius so much that the king introduced yet another new structure. Perhaps you've worked for somebody like that, who's constantly introducing new structures. Perhaps you've been in a church with a leader like that. It's exhausting and also quite threatening.

The new structure, verse 3, has Daniel at the top. Remember by now he's in his eighties. Then there's two administrators and then a hundred and twenty satraps. The satraps are not best pleased by this development. So, verse 4, 'At this, the administrators and the satraps tried to find grounds for charges against Daniel in his conduct of government affairs.' Their response is to make Daniel the target of a conspiracy.

Various suggestions have been put forward as to why this is so. Perhaps, quite naturally, they were jealous of Daniel's promotion; perhaps it was fear of their corruption being exposed; perhaps it was something as simple and straightforward as racism. If you look at verse 13, when they go in front of the king, they make a point of saying 'Daniel, who is one of the exiles from Judah'. 'Darius, he's not one of us.' Maybe it is simply a spiritual attack. Daniel is an obvious target for God's enemies and they try to bring him down. Verse 4, if you like, is the first recorded exercise in tabloid journalism. Digging through someone's dustbin, searching for some bit of gossip, they keep him under surveillance and dig for the dirt. But the one thing that they were not reckoning with was the person and character of Daniel himself.

DANIEL'S CV (VERSE 5)

'They could find no corruption in him, because he was trustworthy and neither corrupt nor negligent.' What an amazing description of somebody who's lived by faith, trusted in God, and who is now in his eighties. For these Hebrews in exile, wondering how involved they could get in the alien world and culture around them, Daniel's example would have rocked them back on their heels. Here was somebody who was right in at the heart of government and yet was not corrupt or negligent. He was trustworthy.

I wonder what people, in your work place, would say about you? Would they be able to describe you as 'neither corrupt nor negligent'? Are you someone like Daniel who gets promotion because you do your job so well, so impressively and so conscientiously that the bosses can do nothing else apart from promote you because they trust you? Or are you singled out because you're a Christian in the work place and that simply means that you're odd? Does being a Christian mean that you don't go to that party, or that drinks do? At times that may well be right. But are you being salt and light where you work, where you probably spend eighty per cent of your time? Thousands of years after Daniel, the apostle Paul would write to the Colossian Christians, 'and whatever you do, whether in word or in deed, do it all in the name of the Lord Jesus, giving thanks to God the Father through him.'

Note, he did not write: 'and whatever you do, whether in the homegroup, or leading the worship or preaching a sermon, or teaching in the children's groups, do it all the name of the Lord Jesus.' This does not apply simply to what we do in the sphere of church; this applies to our whole lives.

Do you do everything 'in the name of the Lord Jesus' in your work place? In the school where you teach? In the office where you work? In the company car you drive? In the hospital where you work as a cleaner or as a doctor, as a radiotherapist or a physiotherapist or a psychologist, whatever it might be? As you spend time with your children in the kitchen or in the playroom? As you work in a factory or as you work in a church?

About twenty years ago, in *The Gravedigger File*,[9] Os Guinness gave a penetrating summary of the problem many of us have when it comes to sharing our faith and being Christians in the workplace. He said, 'The problem is not that Christians are not where they should be. It is that they're not what they should be where they are.'

There's a true story that came out of IFES, the worldwide student movement, in the early 1990s. With the fall of communism, a recent graduate, in a former Soviet bloc country, joined the civil service in his country. He'd been converted to Christ at university and now, in his first year after graduation, he was working in the legal department of the civil service. His immediate boss received a request, direct from their new president, to draft legislation that would severely restrict the freedom of movement and worship of Christians in that new country. His boss, with a wry sense of humour, gave the Christian the job of drafting the legislation that concerned the Christians. This young man had been a Christian perhaps for two years and didn't know what to do. It was the dilemma that he'd hoped and prayed would never happen and there it was on his desk. He prayed, he talked with other people, and he thought for many days.

In the end, he had the courage to request an interview with the president himself. He stood in front of the president of this new nation and said, 'I regret, Mr President, that I cannot be party to drawing up legislation that will have such drastic consequences for my brothers and sisters in Christ. I refuse to do so.' The president apparently looked at him, for what seemed like an age, thought, smiled and then promoted him immediately. He could see that this was a man of integrity, he could see that this was a person who could be trusted and he could see that his government would be better with him in it than with him outside it.

Daniel was by now an old man of such integrity and his contemporaries hated him for it. So we read in verses 7-9 that they persuaded the king to pass this law that nobody should pray to any man or God during the next thirty days. You'd think that somebody at some point would have said, 'Hang on, didn't somebody try this before? Isn't there a furnace around here somewhere? Anybody remember three guys called Shadrach, Meshach and the other bloke?' Nobody did and so they make this proposal to the king.

- *To what extent do you think you have been a good advert for Christianity in your workplace? How have your work colleagues responded to your Christian faith and values?*

DANIEL'S RESPONSE (VERSE 10)

Daniel isn't directly confrontational. He doesn't demand a meeting with Darius. He simply 'went home to his upstairs room where the windows opened toward

Jerusalem. Three times a day he got down on his knees and prayed, giving thanks to his God, just as he had done before.'

Walter Wink, in his comments on these verses, makes this point: 'This seemingly innocuous act was more revolutionary than outright rebellion would have been. Rebellion simply acknowledges the absoluteness and ultimacy of the emperor's power and attempts to seize it. Prayer denies that ultimacy all together by acknowledging a higher power.'

What would your response have been in that situation? Would it have been to become distressed, anxious, to panic or perhaps, like Daniel, to go home and pray?

Maybe the question for some of us is this – *are we cultivating the same habits that Daniel had cultivated in his life?* It was his practice to pray three times a day, at that window open towards Jerusalem. Remember, by now, there was no temple in Jerusalem. With the Hebrews in Babylon there was no longer a priesthood, there was no liturgy. There was no coming together for corporate worship. It's interesting that God uses somebody who certainly is not a member of the professional clergy to further his purposes and extend his kingdom. But, simply, we have an eighty-year-old man of faith, wisdom and cultivated habits who did not change even with the threat of death.

Think about those habits. If somebody was to take a survey of your life, or of the past seven days, would they find regular times in your life when you pray? Perhaps you could subscribe to a website that will send you a piece of Scripture to meditate on. The London Institute for Contemporary Christianity will do that once a week.[10] Have you ever thought about practising some of the spiritual disciplines? If not, then read *The Life You've Always Wanted*[11] by John Ortberg or, if you really want something tough, *The Spirit of the Disciplines*[12] by Dallas Willard.

Every year I try to give myself a spiritual health check. I try when I'm on holiday to re-read the same book, it's called *Restoring Your Spiritual Passion*[13] by Gordon Macdonald. I take time to reflect 'How has my spiritual life grown or how has it slumped in the past twelve months? Where is God challenging me to be different and to devote my energy and my time? Where have I let things slip over the past year?' Each of us needs to develop habits that help us to grow as Christians.

I think it is John Ortberg's contention that if you were to ask people as they leave church on a Sunday morning, 'Do you want to become more like Christ this week?', ninety-nine per cent of people will say, 'Yes.' If you then ask them a supplementary question, 'How is it going to happen? a hundred per cent will say, 'Um...' We plan for many things in life, why don't we plan for our spiritual growth? These habits sustained Daniel.

- *Think about your lifestyle and routine, what habits (holy or otherwise) are you cultivating? How can you plan for spiritual growth?*

Verse 13, we see that Daniel is betrayed.

> 'Daniel, who is one of the exiles from Judah, pays no attention to you, O king, or to the decree you put in writing. He still prays three times a day.' When the king heard this, he was greatly distressed; he was determined to rescue Daniel and made every effort until sundown to save him.

Eventually the king gave the order, verse 16, 'and they brought Daniel and threw him into the lions' den. The king said to Daniel, "May your God, whom you serve continually, rescue you!"'

We know how the story unfolds. The stone is put over the lions' den, the king has a sleepless night and then

'I'm a Christian, get me out of here.'

(v19), at the first light of dawn, 'the king got up and hurried to the lions' den. When he came near the den, he called in an anguished voice to Daniel' – and there are echoes here of the resurrection – '"Daniel, servant of the living God, has your God, whom you serve continually, been able to rescue you from the lions?"'

Then the king almost jumped out of his skin, as a voice replied, 'O king, live forever! My God sent his angel, and he shut the mouths of the lions. They have not hurt me, because I was found innocent in his sight.' Daniel is saved through a crisis but not from a crisis. He is put in the lions' den. Daniel must have felt fear as he looked at those lions and they licked their lips. He wasn't some superhuman, superspiritual, super saint. He must have felt fear but he was delivered through a crisis. Most of us, if we were in Daniel's situation, would have prayed, 'I'm a Christian, get me out of here.' Daniel didn't. He experienced God's power and protection in the lions' den and it wasn't because he knew that for time ever after this story would be useful to Sunday school teachers. He felt real fear and he was protected through the crisis.

What lions are you facing at the moment? Have you been praying for God to take you out of that lions' den? That may be right, in your situation. I don't know what your situation is, but perhaps some of you need to start praying for strength from God to take you through the crisis and to demonstrate God's provision, protection and grace in the crisis and the way in which you deal with it and react to it. It might be in the workplace, it might be in a relationship. But here we have Daniel, a man of faith and integrity, a man of prayer, tact and wisdom, a man who achieved great things for God and with God, a man who saw kings come and kings go and a man who saw God do extraordinary things; above all, a man who knew God in very tough circumstances.

Maybe you need to remember that God is with you as you face those lions. Or perhaps you need to realise that where you work is your place of witness. What do you do if you're going to communicate with an unreached people group, such as accountants? You live with the tribe, you learn their language, you learn their customs and you communicate the gospel in a way they can understand. Some of you may be called, not to an unreached people group, but to people who are cleaners, school teachers, nurses or accountants. That is your unreached people group. And you say, 'I've blown it so many times with my work colleagues.' God is able to give you a fresh start and a new beginning, if only you'll be honest with him, honest with yourself and honest with those that you work with, work for or perhaps who work for you.

- *Think back over your career. How has God used work situations, and even crises, to teach you more about himself? Consider, for example, what you've learnt from times of unemployment, betrayal by a colleague, mounting pressure, standing against corruption and having to juggle work and home life.*
- *Consider your future and the rest of your working life. What do you want to achieve in these years? What do you believe God's priorities are for you in these years? Can you match your goals with God's? Are there changes in attitude, actions, or even place of work you need to make?*

FURTHER STUDY
What kind of work will we be doing in heaven? Look at Luke 19:11-26; Jude 14-15; and Revelation 2:26-27, 5:9-10, 7:9-10 for some ideas.

REFLECTION AND RESPONSE

'The problem is not that Christians are not where they should be. It is that they're not what they should be where they are.' Consider how Os Guinness' words apply to you and your work situation.

- In what ways do you need God's help to be more like salt and light at work?
- Is there a particular work-related situation or issue you need to pray about?
- Who are you praying for at work? Whose salvation are you praying regularly for?

Share with the group any important decisions, meetings, or events coming up at work this week. Spend time praying for these issues as a group and then individually at regular intervals throughout the week. If possible, email or phone group members to let them know how God answered their prayers for you.

POINTS TO PONDER

- What have you learnt about God?
- What have you learnt about yourself?
- What actions or attitudes do you need to change as a result?

PETER MAIDEN
The current Chairman of the Keswick Convention and International Director of Operation Mobilisation, Peter is a very busy man! He travels extensively to fulfil his commitments with OM – overseeing the day-to-day co-ordination of its ministry in 82 countries worldwide. Peter is also an elder at Hebron Evangelical church in Carlisle, where he lives, and manages to include itinerant Bible teaching in the UK and overseas in his schedule. Peter enjoys family life with his wife Win and their three children and grandchildren.

CHAPTER 6

The eternal presence

by Peter Maiden

Aim: To bring our concerns to God and trust in his eternal purpose

> **FOCUS ON THE THEME**
> Look at the list below. Which concerns do you find easy to bring to God and trust him with and which do you find more difficult?
> – Your children
> – Your parents
> – Your health
> – Your future
> – Your job
> – Your daily needs
> – Your struggles with sin
> – Your frustrations with your own personality
> – Your anxiety
> – Your reputation
> – Your financial security
>
> If you are able, explain your answer to the group.

Read: Daniel 8:15–9:24
Key verses: Daniel 9:1-23

As we've been working through this book, we've found Daniel to be a man of God, a man with a heart for God and certainly a heart for God's people. What do you do, when that is your heart, and everything seems to be falling apart around you? Let's face it; life gets like that from time to time. Life seemed to be falling apart around Daniel. In chapters 7 and 8 he had received two visions and he was troubled. At the end of chapter 8 he is a man with many questions and deep concerns.

Gabriel interprets the second dream for him but while his explanation may have dealt with some of Daniel's questions, I don't think it dealt with them all. And it left Daniel still deeply concerned. Look at chapter 8 verse 27, 'I was exhausted and lay ill for several days.' So here's a man so concerned by God's revelation to him that his concern is producing physical symptoms. Some time passes as we move from the end of chapter 8 into chapter 9 but I still wonder whether it was not those deep concerns, those real questions, that led Daniel to the Bible study we find him engaged in at the beginning of chapter 9. Regular time with God, which I'm sure included time in the word of God, had become a discipline, a sacred habit in Daniel's life. It was by now Daniel's natural response, at times of questioning and deep concern, to come to God. If only that could be my normal response, not the last thing I do when I've tried everything else, or the thing I finally do when life becomes unbearable. If only prayer could only be my first, my natural reaction.

- *What is your first natural reaction when you have concerns and questions about your faith?*

In Psalm 73 Asaph is looking around his world and seeing what we so often see when we look around at our world today. The wicked, or at least some of them, are apparently prospering and they're strutting around, very proud of their

The eternal presence

achievements and very patronising about those attempting to lead godly lives and not doing half as well as them. Asaph is confused, as many before him and since him have been. He's struggling with the energy-sapping issue of envy. It all becomes so serious that he says, 'My feet were slipping, I was close to the edge of the cliff.' For him the questions, the doubts, the concerns are so deep, that he's ready to throw away his faith. But listen to this, 'Then one day, I went into the sanctuary, the presence of God ...'

Read the rest of the Psalm and you'll see that one decision just to bring his questions, his concerns, his doubts before God changes everything. His whole perspective on the issues causing him such struggle changes immediately when he finally drags himself, with his questions and his doubts, into the presence of the eternal God. The eternal perspective transforms everything and it appears, on this occasion at least, to do so with immediate effect.

In chapter 9 of Daniel, we find this troubled man, in the presence of God. What's he doing? He's studying the writings of the prophets and particularly the prophet Jeremiah. Never forget the safest place to go, particularly when you find yourself in trouble, is to God and his word. If your world is troubled, learn to go to the Sovereign who rules the world. Our Sovereign God and Father has explained his purposes for the world and for his people in the world. We need to study what God has to say and rely on it. If I rely on my emotions at such times, I'm in double trouble. The words of my friends can often be a great help but the only totally reliable place to go is to God and to his word. That's what Daniel does and his study of Jeremiah brings a surge of excitement, hope and expectation.

Remember the situation that God's people were in when Jeremiah wrote what Daniel was reading. Five hundred and ninety-seven years before Christ, three thousand Jews had been exiled to Babylon, during the reign of King Nebuchadnezzar. And it wasn't long before the false prophets got busy back in Jerusalem and Babylon as well. Often the best days for false prophets are hard days for the people of God. In Jerusalem and Babylon, their message was always the same; it was one long announcement of good news. The false prophets said, 'Tell them what they want to hear, it won't be long before you're home. Babylon will fall sooner rather than later, your exile will be short lived.' Jeremiah hears all of this and immediately writes a letter to the exiles, you'll find it in Jeremiah 29. Basically Jeremiah says, 'Rubbish, rubbish; don't listen to a word of what the false prophets are saying. Instead, build your homes, plan to stay around, get married – only to your own people of course – but have children, grandchildren because your exile's going to last, it's not shortlived. It's going to last for seventy years.' Jeremiah actually gives some very interesting instructions to the people of God. He says this, 'Work for the peace and the prosperity of Babylon. Pray to the Lord for the city where you're held captive. For if Babylon has peace, so will you.'

As we look at the life of Daniel we see how totally obedient to that instruction he was. But you can imagine Daniel's reaction, as he's studying this letter. 'Seventy years. Now, when did that period of time begin? When will it end? How close is our deliverance?' The episode we're studying probably took place about fifty years after the fall of Jerusalem but Daniel's own captivity and exile took place in 604 BC and if that was the starting date for the seventy years, it must almost be over. But as Daniel went on studying, I think much more than dates encouraged him. Why were these false prophets so wrong to predict an early end to the exile? Because it was the Lord who brought about that exile; he had his purpose in it and that purpose was not yet complete. Listen to what

The eternal presence

Jeremiah actually wrote, Jeremiah 29:4. 'This is what the Lord Almighty, the God of Israel, says to all those I carried into exile from Jerusalem to Babylon.' Nebuchadnezzar thought he was involved in this, but God said 'I put my people into exile, I sent them to Babylon from Jerusalem.' Here in Daniel 9:14, we read these words 'The Lord did not hesitate to bring the disaster upon us.'

No doubt the Israelites were feeling forgotten, overrun by the might of Babylon. Was God interested in them anymore? If he was, did he have the power to do anything about their predicament? All the false prophets can say is, 'Keep your chin up, lads, Babylonian power won't last forever, these empires always come and go, you know, you'll be home before you know it.' 'Nonsense,' says Jeremiah. 'The exile has only to do with Babylonian power to the point that the Lord Almighty will use that power to fulfil his purpose.'

I want to ask you honestly, do you believe that sort of thing?

I don't know if you know much about the growth of the church in China but if you look at a graph of the growth of the church it is very level right through the twentieth century and up until about 1970 and then the graph takes off and goes through the roof. I've often wondered, 'What happened around 1970 to cause the sensational growth of the church in China which still goes on today?' I could never get an answer from anyone until I met a Chinese Christian leader and he said, 'The answer to the conundrum is Chairman Mao. Chairman Mao was used of God to cause the growth of the church in China. Of the missionaries, the Christian leaders,' he said

> The missionaries, the Christian leaders, had two problems. One was all the Christians, along with the missionaries, were living on the coastal areas. So no one was going inland with the gospel, they had seminars encouraging it

but nothing happened. And then Chairman Mao, with one edict, caused the mass movement of population. There was much pain, much suffering but, as in the Acts of the Apostles, those Christians went inland, gossiping the gospel as they went. Then the big problem for those who were converted was praying for their ancestors. How could they break that cultural practice? Chairman Mao comes along and thinks he's putting religion to death. He says, 'It'll stop this praying for ancestors overnight; if anyone's found doing it – punishment.'

Those two things, according to my friend, were crucial to the massive growth of the church in China. Chairman Mao was used in the hands of our sovereign God to achieve his purpose.

There are only about three thousand Christians in Turkey. It's a massive country, with only about three thousand evangelical Christians, from a Turkish background. For most, if not the vast majority of those who've come to Christ, an important part of the process has been studying a Bible correspondence course. So the Christians who run this correspondence course wanted to get it advertised on television. The television company, of course, said, 'No, no way, we're not advertising Bible correspondence courses on this channel.' So they produced a programme to tell the people of Turkey how terrible this Bible correspondence course was and how they shouldn't go near it. You know what human beings do when they watch a programme like that? There were more people studying the word of God after that programme then there ever would have been through an advert.

Do we really believe in the sovereign purposes of God, even over the nations? Can God work out his purposes in the chaos in Iraq? What about the struggles in my life? What about the struggles in your life? Can he work out

The eternal presence

his purposes? This exile was in the purpose of God and as with all the purposes of God, it was ultimately for the good of his people. You'll remember Jeremiah 29:11, a favourite verse to so many, 'For I know the plans I have for you,' says the Lord, 'plans to prosper you and not to harm you, plans to give you hope and a future.' Never forget the context when you're quoting that verse. It's not a promise of an easy, trouble-free existence. It was written to a people who were in painful exile and the exile was far from over but God is saying to them, 'Apparent disaster in my sovereign hand is no disaster. I am the sovereign Lord. I'm working for your good in the middle of the pain.'

- *What does trusting in the sovereign purposes of God mean for you right now?*
- *Why does God use pain, hardship and exile experiences to achieve his eternal purpose?*

As Daniel studies the word, his hope is revived but you can also see that he's driven to serious prayer. This man will be a doer of the word, not just a hearer. Yes, he's encouraged by the promise in Jeremiah 29:11 but he sees the promise is conditional on obedience. Listen to verse 12, 'Then you will call upon me and come and pray to me and I will listen to you. You will seek me and find me when you seek me with all your heart. I will be found by you and will bring you back from captivity.' Again, it's good to realise every time you quote that famous promise the context for Israel. The fulfillment of that glorious promise was contingent upon them earnestly seeking the Lord and Daniel immediately sets himself to do this. But remember seeking God in prayer is not just Daniel's knee-jerk reaction in a time of crisis. Long ago it had become the regular practice of his life. He's probably over eighty years of age by this time; he'd been a man of prayer from his youth. I'm sure the devil had tried many times to break the habit. But the seduction of the luxuries of the court of Nebuchadnezzar hadn't been able to break Daniel's reliance upon God and neither had the pressure of the prestige of high office. The path into the presence of God had become a well-worn path for Daniel.

You can imagine, at this moment, the turmoil of his emotions: on the one hand feelings of devastation when that frightening vision had been explained at the end of chapter 8; on the other hand this sense of hope and new possibilities as he reads Jeremiah's letter and responds to the word of God. What does he do with all of this? He brings it down that well-worn path into the presence of the sovereign Lord, whose word and will he knows will be accomplished. God's word, through Jeremiah, called for an earnest seeking after God. So Daniel prepared himself. Not for two quick minutes, rushing into God's presence; he prepares himself to do serious business. Verse 3: he turns to the Lord and pleads in prayer, fasting, and wearing rough sackcloth and ashes. The fasting is Daniel's commitment to real concentration in prayer. He's pleading with God on his own behalf and on behalf of his people. It was a serious matter. These outward expressions of humbling himself, the sackcloth and the ashes, may well have been a real help to Daniel in attaining the right state of mind to seek God. Yes, God is sovereign, yes, he will do as he pleases and yes, his promise is to bless his people. But there's no way that releases Daniel, nor does it release us, from the serious commitment to prayer.

- *How do you get yourself into 'the right state of mind to seek God'?*

As I read this, I find myself immediately asking, 'How much time do I honestly give to the sort of serious prayer commitment modelled by Daniel?' I guess for me there are at least two dangers and they come at the opposite ends of

The eternal presence

the spectrum. God is sovereign, his will shall be done, do I really need to pray? Oh, of course I'll go through the motions because I'm an evangelical, after all. So I'll have my daily prayer time, I'll attend the prayer meeting at the church but am I serious in my prayer commitment, as modelled here by Daniel? The other danger for me, and it's a bigger danger because I'm an activist by nature, is actually to feel I don't need to pray because I can do what needs to be done myself. Again, of course I'll go through the motions of prayer. I'll never have a business meeting, for example, without asking God's blessing at the end and sometimes even at the beginning. 'Please God bless my plans, bless my actions, I can do it with a little help from you. God, you are the builder but actually I can fix it.' I wonder how our all-wise God actually feels about being brought in at the conclusion of our meetings, being asked only to bless our plans. Have you ever thought what a waste it is to rely on human wisdom when his wisdom is one hundred per cent available?

- *How would you answer the question 'God is sovereign, his will shall be done, so do I really need to pray?' What value is prayer to us and to God?*
- *Paul tells us to 'pray continually' (1 Thes. 5:17). What does this mean and how can you do it?*

There's a vital balance here, isn't there? Daniel is a man who clearly trusts in the sovereignty of God but a man who, nevertheless, shows throughout his life and particularly at this time of crisis, an absolute commitment to the serious business of prayer. So having watched Daniel prepare for prayer, let's very briefly look at the prayer itself. It is a wonderful pattern of how prayer should be.

Remember it was the mention of dates, in Jeremiah's letter, which initially brought Daniel into the presence of God. But once he's there, there's no mention of dates. In the presence of God huge issues fill Daniel's mind. It's clear that Daniel's overwhelming concern in prayer is for the glory of God. It takes us back to the model prayer Jesus gave in his prayer seminar. Remember how he said we must begin and we must make our primary petition, 'Hallowed be your name.' Every other petition must be in submission to that primary petition. 'So if it hallows your name to give me my daily bread then so be it, but if not, I'll do without my bread today because my overriding concern is to see your name hallowed.' That is so clearly Daniel's concern in prayer. He glorifies God himself. Verse 4, 'Oh, Lord, the great and awesome God.' Verse 7, 'Lord, you are righteous.' Verse 9, 'You're merciful and forgiving.'

Notice how he says, 'The exile glorifies God.' The nation of Judea had been clearly instructed in the truth of God and by practising idolatry and immorality they'd been defying God to punish them. If God hadn't punished them he would not have been true to his word. So rather than being some sort of disaster Daniel explains the exile is 'a display of the justice of God, proving again that God is faithful to his word, that he does fulfil his promises of judgement as well as mercy.' Look at verses 12 to 14, 'You've done exactly what you warned you would do against us and our rulers. Never, in all history, has there been a disaster like the one that happened in Jerusalem. Every curse written against us in the Law of Moses has come true, all the troubles he predicted, they've all taken place.' By the way, what a solemn word that is for cultures and nations which arrogantly appear to be defying God to punish them today.

Daniel says, 'The exile, rather than being a disaster, is a display of your faithfulness, it brings glory to you.' It's in that conviction, the conviction of the glory, sovereign power and utter faithfulness of God, that Daniel comes with confidence to plead for God's mercy on his people.

The eternal presence

He knows they're towards the end of the seventy years and he comes pleading for mercy. 'In view of all your faithful mercies,' that's the faithful mercies of the exile, 'please turn your furious anger away from your city of Jerusalem' (v16). But notice again Daniel's primary plea is for the glory of God. He doesn't want God's name to be dishonoured. He reports to God, 'All the neighbouring nations mock Jerusalem and your people because of our sins and the sins of our ancestors' (v16). Look at the middle of verse 18, 'See how our city lies in ruins and everyone knows it's your city. We don't ask because we deserve help but because you're merciful. Oh Lord hear. Oh Lord forgive. Oh Lord, listen and act for your own sake. Oh my God, don't delay.' What an example Daniel is to all of us of priority in prayer. I find, so easily, in my own prayer life that it becomes a very selfish exercise. Not so for Daniel. His primary motivation is the glory of God. Even as he requests mercy after these seventy years of exile, it's not primarily for his own sake or for his people's sake, it's for the glory of God. And I can only say to you that I have a great deal personally to learn from Daniel on this point.

- *How can we bring God glory? For some examples, look at John 11:1-4, 15:8, 17:6-10.*
- *What does praying for the glory of God mean in your own situation?*

So here's Daniel deeply distressed and greatly burdened about the visions he's seen. But as you look at the prayer, you can see that although his concerns are great, his confidence in God is absolute. Surely this is the great secret of Daniel's prayer; complete confidence in God. And that confidence is expressed in the names Daniel uses to address God. One of our OM teams was helping out in an orphanage in Africa recently. They were using the Lord's prayer to teach English and the great day came for the children to show how much they'd learned. One little fellow got up and said, 'Our Father, who art in heaven. Hello, what's your name?' The names of God are extremely important. Look at verse 3. 'So I turned to the Lord God,' that's Adonai Elohim, the Mighty God, Sustainer of all things. But then look at verse 4, 'I prayed to the Lord my God,' Jehovah Elohim; the covenant God of his own people. And that's Daniel's conviction. God is the Almighty One, he's able to do all things and he remains committed to his people. They may be exiled from the sacred soil of Israel because of disobedience but Daniel boldly claims Yahweh's mercy, as the covenant-keeping God.

Before Daniel has finished praying, Gabriel appears again. Verse 23, 'The moment you began praying, a command was given.' Isn't that fabulous? The moment he began praying, God began to take action. Many have said before me, and I'm sure it's true, that the Lord is far more ready to answer our prayers than we are to ask. Gabriel encourages Daniel with a promise, in verse 24, 'A period of seventy sets of seven has been decreed for your people and your holy city, to put down rebellion, to bring an end to sin, to atone for guilt, to bring in everlasting righteousness, to confirm the prophetic vision and to anoint the most holy place.' Then Gabriel continues with details of how those seventy sets of seven will work.

I don't have time to explain those details to you. But as with many prophecies, there's certainly a twofold fulfilment. The fulfilment would be seen over the next four hundred and ninety years of Israel's history, the seven sets of seventy. Any good Bible commentary will show you how, in the next four hundred and ninety years of the nation's history, this promise was fulfilled. But it must be clear, to all who read these verses, that what happened in those four hundred and ninety years of Israel's history can in no way explain fully what's being predicted here. For example, just look at that first promise of Gabriel. 'A day is coming,' says Gabriel, 'which will bring an

The eternal presence

end to sin or rebellion against God.' The true fulfilment of that prophecy requires the inauguration of the kingdom of God on this earth. That's the vital point that Gabriel is making. 'Daniel, you're concerned for the state of your people and yes, God's covenant with his people is not annulled. You'll see that faithfulness over the next four hundred and ninety years of their history but there's a bigger picture. God is in control of that far bigger picture, he will be in control right to the end of time and to that day when an end to sin will be brought in.'

How vital it is always to have that bigger picture before us. We need to be able to look away from our immediate issues, our present struggles and see the God who is in control of all things, the whole of world history. We know that the One who is in control of the whole of world history is in control of your world and of my world. So what are your struggles, doubts and questions? The only safe place to bring such doubts, to bring such questions, is to God, into his eternal presence and there those problems may well be seen in an entirely different perspective. Remember you're coming into the presence of the One who is in control of world history. You're coming into the presence of the One who can lead to the growth of the church in China through Chairman Mao and use him to fulfil his purposes. God is in control of my world and yours. He's our God, committed to us by covenant, working out his purposes for good, even in the middle of pain and confusion.

I think some of us have very little difficulty trusting the Lord with the management of the universe but, if we're honest, we feel our personal situation is a bit more complex, a little more difficult. We're very anxious and troubled about the management of our lives. Let's take a stand together. Let's stand on the power and the trustworthiness of God. Whatever the issues in our lives, let's be determined to take a stand and trust in his power and grace. But as we do so, remember he calls us to seek him with all our hearts and if we have strayed from him, to return wholeheartedly to him.

- *Look at the following passages which give us a big-picture perspective, an overview, of key truths:*
  - *Job 38:1-41 – God's control over creation*
  - *Psalm 139:1-16 – God's intimate knowledge of us*
  - *1 Thessalonians 5:1-11 – The certainty of the Second Coming*
  - *Colossians 1:19-23 – The reality of our salvation*
  - *2 Corinthians 4:7-18 –The value of suffering*

How do these passages help us deal with our concerns and questions? How do they help us adjust our perspective to a one that trusts God and his eternal purposes?

FURTHER STUDY

The names of God are important because they tell us about his character and attributes. Daniel's prayer mentions some of the names of God but what are the others? Look up the names of God in a Bible dictionary. List the different names you find and meditate on each one.

God's name was also used to commemorate events or places in the Old Testament. For example:

- Jehovah Jireh – The Lord provides – Genesis 22:8, 14
- Yahweh nissi – The Lord is my banner – Exodus 17:15
- Jehovah shalom – The Lord is peace – Judges 6:24
- Jehovah shammah – The Lord is there – Ezekiel 48:35

Look up these references and the surrounding verses. What comfort and encouragement do these passages offer for your own situation?

REFLECTION AND RESPONSE

Bring your struggles and concerns to God. Determine to trust him even though the situation may look bleak. Trust he is working everything out according to his sovereign plan and eternal purpose. Make Daniel's prayer your own:

'We do not make requests of you because we are righteous, but because of your great mercy. O Lord, listen! O Lord, forgive! O Lord, hear and act! For your sake, O my God, do not delay, because your city and your people bear your Name' (Dan. 9:18b-19).

As a group, follow Daniel's example and ask God's forgiveness for the sins of our nation. Pray that God will be merciful and restore the honour of his Name in our land.

POINTS TO PONDER
- What have you learnt about God?
- What have you learnt about yourself?
- What actions or attitudes do you need to change as a result?

CHAPTER 7

The best is still to come

by Dave Richards

Aim: To cultivate an integrated faith focused on God

FOCUS ON THE THEME
We all have different weaknesses and pressure points. Consider how God has made you tick: what are the typical reasons why you take your eyes off God?

What people, events, spiritual disciplines or daily habits do you need to build into your life to shift your focus back to God? Share with the group what you have learnt about how God has made you.

Read: Daniel 10:1–12:13
Key verses: Daniel 10:1-14, 12:1-13

Have you seen the film *Good Will Hunting*? It's a few years old. It stars Matt Damon and Ben Affleck. Matt Damon plays a maths genius who works as a cleaner in a university. Each day the people who lecture in the maths department leave very complicated and difficult problems on the blackboard for their students to solve. The students can't solve them and the lecturers are mystified when they come to teach classes the next day and a solution is found at the bottom of the blackboard. They just can't understand it. What they don't realise is that it's the cleaner who actually looks at the blackboard and puts the answer at the bottom. Ben Affleck, who plays his friend, tries to persuade him throughout the film to leave his cleaning job to fulfil his potential and to go to university. And in the book, *Second Choice*,[14] Viv Thomas says this about Will, the character played by Matt Damon, 'Will is an angry and broken young man who has not learned to love others or accept himself. He is on the run from himself, living a split life without integration. The film is saying that we do not live well if we deny what we are and seek to be something else.'

If we're honest that's true for many of us as Christians. A lot of the time we actually deny who we are and who God intended us to be, and we seek to be something else. We want, as it were, to have one foot in the kingdom of God and one foot in the world. We wonder sometimes why it doesn't always feel very comfortable. The result is that many Christians lead split lives without integration. They are one thing in church; they are another thing in the workplace. They are one thing in the CU or the youth group; they are something else when they are with their mates in the park or in the classroom. The tragedy is that we believe God is only interested in what we call 'our spiritual lives'. We believe that God isn't actually concerned about everything else that we do – God isn't concerned what we do with our money, he isn't concerned with what we do with our leisure time, he isn't concerned with the clothes that we wear, he isn't concerned with where we go on holiday, he isn't concerned about the ambitions that we have for ourselves or how we act towards the people around us because he is simply interested, so we think, in 'the spiritual things'.

But God is interested in all of our lives, everything we do.

The best is still to come 111

- *Viv Thomas writes, 'We do not live well if we deny what we are and seek to be something else.' In what ways do Christians deny who they are? Why do we seek to be something else?*
- *We imagine that the clothes we wear, where we go on holiday and the ambitions we have for ourselves come fairly low down God's agenda. Why is God interested in these issues? What would he want to say to you about them?*
- *If your faith was more integrated, what changes would other people notice?*

If we're honest, many of us have reduced the Christian faith to what Dallas Willard calls 'barcode Christianity'. In our eagerness to explain the gospel to other people, in our enthusiasm to communicate the Christian faith in a way that people outside the church will understand, we reduce the gospel to 'two ways to live' or 'four spiritual laws'. There is nothing wrong in those outlines, they are good things. But they aren't Christianity. We've reduced the Christian faith to whether you have a barcode on your body. We imagine that when you die, God stands there with a scanner and he passes the scanner over you and if you go 'bleep' you go to heaven and if you don't go 'bleep' you go to hell. Christianity is much more than that. Jesus spoke about coming and giving us life in all its fullness, not four spiritual laws or even two ways to live, good though those gospel outlines are. We should know at least one of them so that we can communicate the Christian faith to other people.

Daniel, as we have seen, was somebody whose life was not split between the sacred and the secular. That's a divide that we have in Western Christianity, especially in the evangelical church in the UK. Today we concentrate on dividing the sacred and the secular rather than thinking about the divide between the sacred and the profane. You can do something that appears spiritual and appears Christian. That doesn't mean that it's sacred; it could actually be profane. You can pray and it can be profane. You can lead a church and it can be profane. You can speak at the Keswick Convention and it can be profane, if it's not done for the right reasons and the right motives.

Viv Thomas said, 'Central to Daniel's ability to live with his givenness was his ability to live with complexity. Daniel had to live with his personal history and the purpose of God for his nation.' The two were intertwined. Complexity is there, from Daniel chapter 1 right through to Daniel chapter 12; the interlocking of the personal and the national, the individual and the global, from the time when he was a young man right through to the time when he was an old person.

Look at the first six chapters. There is so much going on at a national level. In chapter 1:1, 2, Israel was led into exile. In chapter 2, Nebuchadnezzar has a dream. In chapter 4:1-8, Nebuchadnezzar has another dream. In Chapter 5:1-16, Belshazzar hosts a meal. In chapter 6:1-9, there is political infighting. All this is going on at a national level. But intertwined with these events is Daniel's personal life. In chapter 1:6-10 Daniel, Shadrach, Meshach and Abednego are picked for stardom. In chapter 2:17-23, we have Daniel's prayer. In chapter 4:19-27 and 5:17-31 Daniel interprets the royal dreams. In chapter 6:10-28 we see Daniel's integrity. In chapters 7–9 Daniel's personal life is again woven in with national concerns and events; his life is inextricably linked with the life of the people of God. In chapter 7:2-27, history is foretold. Daniel has this amazing vision of what will happen over the next few hundred years in the history of the world. In chapter 8:5-26 he has another vision where history is foretold. And in chapter 9:4-27 we have Daniel's prayer for his nation, the people of God, and God's answer.

The best is still to come   113

So we come to chapters 10–12 and this is the largest single section in the book. It's a very wordy section. If you look at chapters 7–9 you will see that what characterises them is pictures and visions. But chapters 10-12 are slightly different. It's *Test Match Special* as opposed to Channel 4's cricket coverage. It's *The Times* as opposed to *Hello!* magazine. Again, there is a very clear structure. Firstly, chapter 10:1 through to chapter 11:1 is the introduction. Secondly, chapter 11:2 to chapter 12: 4 is the revelation that Daniel is given. Then in chapter 12:5-13, we have the epilogue.

Let's look at the introduction: 'In the third year of Cyrus king of Persia, a revelation was given to Daniel (who was called Belteshazzar). Its message was true and it concerned a great war' (10:1).

What have we learned from this verse? Several things: firstly, it gives us the setting. We are in the third year of the reign of Cyrus, the king of Persia. Secondly, we are told that it's a revelation. Thirdly, we are told that it came to Daniel. Fourthly, we are told that its message was true. Fifthly, we are told that it concerned a great war.

And Daniel understands the message that he is given in chapter 10 through this angelic visitation. He's been fasting (v3), 'I ate no choice food; no meat or wine touched my lips; and I used no lotions at all until the three weeks were over.' He wasn't exfoliating, he wasn't moisturizing; he was simply waiting upon God.

> On the twenty-fourth day of the first month, as I was standing on the bank of the great river, the Tigris, I looked up and there before me was a man dressed in linen, with a belt of the finest gold around his waist. His body was like chrysolite, his face like lightning, his eyes like flaming torches, his arms and legs like the gleam of burnished bronze, and his voice like the sound of a multitude (v4-6).

We aren't told who this is. There are similarities with the description of Gabriel in chapter 9:21. There are, for many of us, hints of the book of Revelation and John's vision of the Risen Jesus in Revelation 1:13-16. But we aren't told exactly who this is. We can guess, but it's only a guess. Who it is isn't important. The significant thing is what he reveals to Daniel.

The main thing that he reveals is that there is a link between the physical realm and the spiritual realm, between what happens here on earth and between that realm wherever it is, where God, Jesus, the angels and the devil and demons exist. There's a link between the two. The speaker told him:

> Do not be afraid, Daniel. Since the first day that you set your mind to gain understanding and to humble yourself before your God, (again an insight into how Daniel approached prayer) your words were heard, and I have come in response to them. But the prince of the Persian kingdom resisted me twenty-one days. Then Michael, one of the chief princes, came to help me, because I was detained there with the king of Persia. Now I have come to explain to you what will happen to your people in the future, for the vision concerns a time yet to come (v12-14).

Those three verses alone have caused all sorts of difficulties to all sorts of preachers and to all sorts of churches. People have disagreed vehemently and fundamentally with each other. I might be wrong and feel free to disagree with me, because it's not exactly clear. But maybe what is being referred to here is this link between the physical and the spiritual realm; that what happens on earth is influenced by what happens in the heavenlies and vice versa. But, as soon as I say those words, for some of you, alarm bells will start to ring and we do need to be very careful. In the past twenty to thirty years, along with the charismatic movement, there has been a huge explosion of interest in the whole topic of spiritual warfare in the United Kingdom. There have been many books written, many seminars given, lots of things said and done, prayed and sung, cast out and cast in. But is what we have done a reflection of what is here in Scripture or have some people in their enthusiasm departed from what Scripture lays down?

There have been some very good books written on spiritual warfare, which basically means that I agree with them, and there have been awful books written, which basically means that I disagree with them. This whole subject is very popular. I remember, a few years ago, attending Spring Harvest, and going to a seminar in the afternoon on 'Christians in Politics'. There were about forty people in the room. The next seminar in the same room, an hour later, was on spiritual warfare and the numbers swelled from forty to four hundred. It showed where people's priorities lie. Politics, no! Demons, I'm there! You see, there is something exciting, there is something interesting, there is something intriguing about the whole subject. If we are honest, we need to recognise that about spiritual warfare. The word 'occult' literally means 'hidden', and hidden things – forbidden things – hold a fascination and excitement for us. We therefore need to recognise our own motives when talking about this area – even as Christians.

I can tell you that there is nothing exciting or intriguing about this subject. My dad was a spiritualist for about seventeen or eighteen years and it was tragic to see the effect that the occult had upon his life. I used to try to talk to him about my Christian faith but got nowhere until about 1985, during what was his third nervous breakdown. He asked me to get a friend and come and pray with him. We talked about Jesus and that, I think, was the first time in seventeen years he really understood who Jesus was. When it says in 2 Corinthians 4 that 'the God of this age has blinded the hearts and minds of unbelievers', it's true. My dad lived through hell. He experienced things and saw things that, even now, he will not tell me because they were so dreadful.

So this is a real subject. But we need to tread carefully and we need to stick to the guidelines that Scripture gives to us. We do need to take it seriously. Daniel 10:13 and Daniel 10:20 reinforce the reality of spiritual warfare. There is a devil, there is evil, there are fallen angels and there is a link between what occurs in the spiritual realm and here on earth. If there isn't a link then what's the point in praying?

In Daniel 10:13, the conflict between Israel and Persia reflects the battle between the Prince of the Persian Kingdom and Michael, one of the chief princes. Elsewhere we know him as an archangel. In Daniel 10:20, the approaching threat to Israel from Greece and Alexander the Great is reflected in the approaching conflict in the spiritual realm between Michael and the Prince of Greece. There seems to be this link in prayer and, somehow, Daniel has been involved in the battle, even though he didn't realise it. Perhaps many of us are involved in that battle without realising. Maybe that's no bad thing.

It was a theme picked up by the Apostle Paul when he wrote to the church at Ephesus, a city full of tremendous occult activity and idolatry. In Ephesians 6:12, Paul writes 'For our struggle is not against flesh and blood'. People who are not Christians are not the enemy, so why do we behave towards them as though they are? Paul says, 'our battle is not against flesh and blood but against the rulers, against the authorities, against the powers of this dark world and against the spiritual forces of evil in the heavenly realms'. In light of that, Paul urges the Ephesian Christians to pray and he urges us to pray. In his commentary on Daniel, Ernest Lucas observes

> There is a synergism between events in heaven and on earth. This doesn't mean that earthly history is simply decided in heaven but human prayer does have its effect on the events concerned. Humans are responsible for what goes on in history but history is not the outworking of human decisions alone.[15]

This world, though it appears to be, is not out of control. God is in charge of our world, he is Sovereign. But we play our part too. We play our part through prayer, amongst other things. If we look at the writings of Paul in the New Testament it strikes me that he is perhaps deliberately vague in the terms that he uses. He uses a whole collection of different words and meanings to describe these principalities and powers. It seems, at times, that the principalities and powers do have something human about them; they're visible, they're structural and they are political. But also there is an aspect to them which is suprahuman: invisible, immaterial and spiritual. Paul is not simply talking about things that are metaphors for earthly structures, which is what some from a more liberal theological perspective think, when he refers to principalities and powers. But neither do these things exist independently of these structures.

What does the Bible say about these principalities and powers? Firstly, Colossians 1:15, 16 tells us they are created entities. The devil, remember, is part of God's creation, he is a created being. Therefore the devil is limited as to what he can do. Most importantly, above everything else, these principalities and powers were disarmed and defeated by Jesus on the cross. Colossians 2:15, 'Having disarmed the powers and authorities, he made a public spectacle of them, triumphing over them by the cross.' One day, at Christ's second coming, they will be destroyed. That should be our focus. These things were defeated by the cross of Jesus Christ and one day they will be destroyed.

The danger of this whole area of spiritual warfare is that we go beyond what the Bible prescribes for us. You may disagree with what I am about to say but these are my opinions, based on what I think Scripture says and about twenty years' experience of praying with people and for people, from time to time as it's occurred. I come from a charismatic background and I've seen some of these extremes worked out in practice.

So, for example, I don't think there is a place for naming particular spirits associated with places or with territories. Daniel is told this as part of the revelation but it's not what he asked God for. Secondly, I don't see any provision in Scripture for wrestling with evil spirits in prayer. Daniel certainly does not do that. He prays to God and he receives a visitation from an angel. But he doesn't wrestle with the Prince of Persia or with the Prince of Greece. Michael, the archangel, does that but Daniel doesn't do it in prayer.

Remembering the devil is a created being, it seems to me there is no room for dualism. To listen to some Christians speak and, especially some charismatic Christians, it's almost as though it's a battle every day between God on one hand and the devil on the other. They're both equally powerful and it's a daily question as to who's going to win. One day it's God and the next day it's the devil and then God gets the next round and then the devil has a little victory here. It is not like that. The devil is a created being, limited in space and time, if you can be limited in space and time, in eternity. He has limited knowledge. He has limited power. We can venture into Satan's territory by repeated and deliberate sin, perhaps by opening ourselves up to the occult if we aren't Christians. We can enter into Satan's territory if we deliberately choose to do that but it is not a question of dualism; the devil and God being equally powerful and us having to wait and see who's going to win.

Neither do I think the Scriptures give any place for a sort of formulaic approach to prayer about these things, binding the devil or claiming people or places. I remember one student in Birmingham University telling me that she had claimed the shower for Jesus. I said, 'What do you expect to happen to people who go into that shower? Will they suddenly be overcome by the presence of God as the water falls down? If they've been particularly naughty or wicked the night before, will the water get really, really, really hot? I mean, what are you expecting to happen?'

It seems also that if you look at Scripture there is no basis for any complicated demonology or spiritual hierarchies. If you look at the life and ministry of Jesus, he did not have a demonology. He simply got rid of them. He didn't make a fuss. He spoke to them like a child who was misbehaving, 'Be quiet, get out.' No singing the right worship song and getting the right atmosphere; he just told them, 'Be quiet, shut up and get out.' No histrionics, he dealt with them and doing so was only part of his ministry. I think we should beware of people who say that they have a ministry of deliverance or organisations that set themselves up as exorcism agencies. It's part of the ministry of the church, but it is only part, because it was part of the ministry of Jesus. Our focus, it seems to me, needs to be on Jesus; on his cross, his resurrection and his victory.

- *To what extent are you aware of the spiritual forces of evil at work?*
- *What can we learn from Revelation 2-3 about how the evil one attacks believers and how we can resist him?*

- *What have you learnt from Daniel about the power of prayer in the spiritual battle? Look particularly at 10:12-13.*
- *How does prayer help you keep your focus on God?*
- *Look at Ephesians 6:10-18 for a godly perspective and balanced approach to evil in the spiritual realms. In practical terms what does the armour of God actually consist of? What does a well-armed Christian look like?*

Daniel prayed to God and focused on God and that's where Daniel as a book ends as well. Chapter 12 and verses 1 to 4 are perhaps the clearest affirmation of resurrection in the Hebrew Bible. 'At that time Michael, the great prince who protects your people, will arise. There will be a time of distress such as has not happened from the beginning of nations until then. But at that time your people – everyone whose name is found written in the book – will be delivered.' Again, it's one of so many instances where you find Revelation hinted at.

> Multitudes who sleep in the dust of the earth will awake: some to everlasting life, others to shame and everlasting contempt. Those who are wise will shine like the brightness of the heavens, and those who lead many to righteousness, like the stars for ever and ever (v2-3).

Paul picks up the imagery of the shining light in Philippians. He speaks of Christians shining like stars in the universe, without fault, in a crooked and depraved generation (Phil. 2:15). The challenge is for you and me to lead lives of faith, integrity and truth – and that are distinctively different from the world in which we live. The challenge is to drive back the forces of darkness not simply by the prayers we pray, but also by the quality of our lives, individually and collectively, which are characterised by love, mercy, grace and truth.

The best is still to come

'But you, Daniel, close up and seal the words of the scroll until the time of the end. Many will go here and there to increase knowledge.' There are going to be wars and conflicts. There are echoes here again of the end of Matthew's gospel, Matthew 24 and 25, with Jesus speaking about the end of time, 'there will be wars and rumours of wars and nation will rise against nation but the end is not then.'

The exile to Babylon will not be the end of Israel's problems. Talk to somebody who is Jewish and ask them about the past two thousand years. The exile in Babylon was not the end of their problems. But the end will come, we don't know how or when, verses 7-10

> The man clothed in linen, who was above the waters of the river, lifted his right hand and his left hand toward heaven, and I heard him swear by him who lives forever, saying, 'It will be for a time, times and half a time. When the power of the holy people has been finally broken, all these things will be completed.'

Like so many people down the centuries, Daniel says for you and for me,

> I heard, but I did not understand. So I asked, 'My lord, what will the outcome of all this be?' He replied, 'Go your way, Daniel, because the words are closed up and sealed until the time of the end. Many will be purified, made spotless and refined, but the wicked will continue to be wicked. None of the wicked will understand, but those who are wise will understand' (v 8-10).

We won't know how, we won't know when, and neither should we trouble ourselves too much with the detail of when Jesus will come, despite some people selling lots of books on the subject. Jesus doesn't know when the Second Coming is going to happen (Mt. 24:36), so why do we think we should? But it will come, it will happen. 'Like a thief in the night', Jesus said, like lightening in the sky, from one side of the sky to the other, no-one will be in any doubt, his Second Coming will be completely different from his First Coming. Our challenge, just like Daniel's, is to live and pray so that the kingdom of God is extended. As we focus on heaven, our goal is to take as many people as possible with us.

The Second Coming is a reality. I was talking just last week with a friend who isn't a Christian. He had been made to think by an article in the *Sunday Times* written about the Le Haye and Jenkins books, the *Left Behind* series that are so popular in America. I've known this guy for about four years, and he said, 'Tell me about the Second Coming of Jesus.' You don't get invitations like that very often and so we talked for half an hour. By the end, he was convinced that it may happen but his last words to me were fascinating. He said, 'Dave, if it happens, and my wife is in the hairdressers', will you come and get me?' I had to say, 'It won't be like that, it will be too late. We'll have actually gone to be with your wife. All that will be left will be a hairdryer because she won't be there any more.' It will happen, but for the Christians, the best is yet to come.

I love the story of an old woman in the Deep South of the United States. She was dying and the pastor was visiting her. He asked her if she had any requests for the funeral – hymns, songs, prayers or readings. She said, 'I've got one request, but it's a bit unusual. I'd like to be buried holding a spoon.' He thought, 'Well, okay, but why?'

Now, in America it's quite common to have the coffin open during the funeral service. A friend of mine conducted a funeral service in a Baptist church in the southern USA and the person who had died was bolt upright. They had propped them upright in the coffin, put their reading glasses on and given them a Bible. He said it was a very eerie feeling, preaching with this person looking over his shoulder.

So, in parts of the US, open coffins are quite common and the old woman had said 'I want to be buried and have the funeral service with the coffin open and a spoon in my hand.' He said 'Why a spoon?' She said, 'Well, do you remember those church suppers when people would come with a salad and whatever and we would have the first course? My favourite bit of those meals was when they would start to clear away the first course and we knew that the pudding was coming because they would tell us, "Keep your spoon." I want to be at that funeral service holding a spoon so that people remember that the best is still to come.' Keep your spoon!

Daniel lived a life of integrity and faith. He prayed consistently and significantly, he lived as a minority in a culture that was foreign and, at times, hostile to his faith. His own life was bound up with the fate of his nation. He was given insight into huge swathes of human history but he remained focused on his God and on that eternal reality.

As you go back to wherever you're going back to, your school or college, the office or hospital where you work, whether you're going to read gas meters or to look after children in the home, even if you're going back to a difficult church with difficult relationships where you're the pastor, let's make a resolve that we go back, as somebody once put it, 'to lead lives that are of such joy and quality that when we die, even the undertakers are sad', and remember, keep your spoon because the best is yet to come.

- *What difference does it make to your life to know that 'the best is still to come'?*
- *How did Daniel cultivate an integrated faith focused on God? What lessons can we learn from him?*

FURTHER STUDY

The Bible does not give us much concrete detail about the future but what can we learn? For example, what events and circumstances will precede the Second Coming, what will Jesus' return to earth be like? Knowing his return could be imminent how should we prepare? For some ideas look at 1 Thessalonians 4:13–5:11, 2 Thessalonians 2:1-17, 2 Timothy 3:1–4:7, 1 Peter 4:7-11, 2 Peter 3:3-18.

REFLECTION AND RESPONSE

Spend time reflecting on what you have learnt from the book of Daniel:

- Do you need to draw some boundary lines in your life?
- Are there areas of your life you have withheld from God's control?
- Are there idols in your life you need to get rid of?
- Do you need to trust more in God's sovereignty?
- Do you need to let the reality of God make more of an impact on your life?
- Do you need to develop your prayer life?
- Do you need to develop a more integrated faith?
- What impact is your faith having on your community, home and workplace?
- How can you keep your focus on eternal realities?

Think through how the book of Daniel has challenged your faith and then decide how God is asking you to respond. If you find it helpful, write down your responses on a piece of paper and keep it in your Bible as a reminder of the commitments you have made. If it is appropriate, pray through these issues with another member of the group. Discuss how you could help each other keep your commitments to God and grow as Christians.

POINTS TO PONDER
- What have you learnt about God?
- What have you learnt about yourself?
- What actions or attitudes do you need to change as a result?

[1] Karl Popper, *The open society and its enemies* (Routledge, 2002) – first published in 1945
[2] Viv Thomas, *Second choice – embracing life as it is* (Carlisle: Paternoster press, 2000)
[3] Ronald Wallace, *Daniel – the Bible speaks today series* (Leicester: IVP, 1984)
[4] Frank Gaebelein, ed. *Expositors Bible Commentary* Vol 7 (Zondervan 1985)
[5] Tremper Longman III, *The NIV Application Commentary: Daniel* (Zondervan 1999)
[6] John White, *The golden cow* (Carlisle: STL, 1980)
[7] John White, *Money isn't God so why is the church worshipping it?* (Leicester: IVP, 1993)
[8] Mark Greene, *Thank God it's Monday* (Bletchley: Scripture Union, 2001)
[9] Os Guinness, *The gravedigger file* (IVP, 1983)
[10] Contact them via their website, www.licc.org.uk
[11] John Ortberg, *The life you've always wanted* (Zondervan, 2002)
[12] Dallas Willard, *The Spirit of the disciplines* (London: Hodder & Stoughton, 1996)
[13] Gordon Macdonald, *Restoring your spiritual passion* (Highland Books, 2004)
[14] Viv Thomas, *Second choice – embracing life as it is* (Carlisle: Paternoster press, 2000)
[15] Ernest Lucas, Daniel: *Apollos Old Testament Commentary Series* (Leicester: IVP, 2002)